DESSERTS AND PASTRIES

By Anne Willan
Illustrated by Chloë Cheese

WALKER BOOKS

To master pâtissiers Albert Jorant and Maurice Ferré
My affectionate thanks

I also acknowledge with pleasure the help of Denise Cassis,
their former student at La Varenne Ecole de Cuisine in Paris.

Designer: Jim Bunker

First published 1988 by Walker Books Ltd
87 Vauxhall Walk, London SE11 5HJ

Printed and bound in Italy
by L.E.G.O., Vicenza

British Library Cataloguing in Publication Data
Willan, Anne, *1938–*
Anne Willan's desserts and pastries.
1. Desserts – Recipes
I. Title
641.8′6
ISBN 0-7445-0771-5
ISBN 0-7445-0715-4 Pbk

CONTENTS

INTRODUCTION

All good cooking, it seems to me, begins at home. I owe my introduction to the kitchen to Emily, our fat old cook; her pastries were a special treat to a child. Despite wartime rations, our teatime table was generously furnished with an array of Yorkshire goodies, from parkin to ribbon pound cake and drop scones. Thursday, baking day, was a paradise of stirring, spoon licking and eating up the crumbs.

When later I joined the Cordon Bleu in London, the variety of fanciful French pastries I found there seemed a natural extension of old Emily's lightness of touch. Pots de crème, after all, were only a refinement on custard tart, and French puff pastry an elaboration of a good flaky dough.

It was when I reached France and worked with an experienced pastry chef, apprenticed in the trade from the age of twelve, that I began to appreciate the intricacies of his exacting art. Measurements must be accurate. The rules of shaping, moulding, chilling and baking must be meticulously followed. The custom of lining a charlotte mould with ladyfingers, or baking madeleines in shell-shaped moulds, is not just convention, but also a key to success.

It is these tricks of such an imaginative and satisfying trade that I try to pass on in this book. I try to show you which corners can be cut and where to take time, when to keep whisking and when to hover, hawk-like, at the oven door.

Like good children, fine pastry and desserts are a matter of love and attention. And both bring incomparable rewards!

Anne Willan

1
HOT SOUFFLES, OMELETTES & SABAYONS

Puffy and brown, rising perilously high above its dish, a soufflé is surely the ultimate symbol of French cuisine. Yet, like many such *tours de force*, it depends less on culinary skill than on understanding the principles involved.

A soufflé consists of two parts: a basic mixture which gives it character, and whipped egg whites which make it rise. Almost all sweet soufflés are based on a mixture of milk, egg yolks, sugar and flour (or arrowroot or cornflour) – in effect a pastry cream (p. 58).

Sought-after exceptions in these days of new-style cuisine are chocolate soufflé, which for body relies only on egg yolks and the chocolate's own richness, and mixtures based on jam or lemon curd, which have enough thickness without the addition of flour.

The classic soufflé dish is purpose-designed and almost indispensable (though in desperation I've cooked soufflés in a charlotte mould and even in a saucepan). Once in the oven, the air in the egg whites expands and the mixture slips up the buttered sides of the mould in a neat straight-sided cylinder to tower like magic above the rim. I'm an advocate of high heat to give the soufflé a quick boost, browning the outside to a crisp crust but leaving the centre soft so that it forms a sauce.

Soufflé omelettes are simplified soufflés, with a basic mixture made of egg yolks beaten with sugar. After adding whipped egg whites, the mixture is too fragile to bake like a true soufflé, so it is cooked in an omelette pan, first on top of the stove and then in the oven or under the grill to brown the top. Filled with jam or fried apples and flamed if you like, a soufflé omelette is the easiest of emergency desserts.

For sabayon the approach is different as the egg yolks, sugar and wine or liqueur are all whipped together over low heat. The French serve sabayon as a sauce, often with cake or a fruit tart. Current favourites are gratins of fresh fruit, coated with sabayon and browned under the grill. Or you may prefer sabayon Italian-style, made with Marsala, and served warm on its own in a stemmed glass.

KEYS TO THE BEST HOT SOUFFLES, OMELETTES AND SABAYONS

The flavouring of a basic soufflé mixture must be concentrated to balance the bland egg whites.

The consistency of the basic soufflé mixture should match that of whipped egg whites as closely as possible. If it is too sticky, the basic mixture glues the soufflé down; if it is too liquid, air is knocked out of the whites during folding.

For detailed instructions on whipping egg whites see Glossary (p. 91).

For sweet soufflés and omelettes, the egg whites are whipped then beaten with sugar to make a light meringue. This holds better than plain egg whites and is easier to mix.

When folding in meringue, add about a quarter to the basic mixture and stir quite thoroughly to give an open texture. If at this point the basic soufflé mixture has been warmed, the meringue is cooked lightly and stays firmer when the remaining meringue is folded in.

Once the egg whites are added, a soufflé should be baked at once, though a well-prepared mixture can wait for an hour or two in the refrigerator without harm. Soufflé omelettes, however, must be cooked at once.

Individual soufflés baked in ramekins are less risky, if less spectacular, than one large soufflé dish.

If you butter the soufflé dish twice, chilling it quickly in between in the freezer, this helps prevent sticking.

Set a soufflé low in the oven, so it has plenty of room to rise.

When done, a soufflé should be well puffed but still concave on top, showing that it is still soft in the centre.

Soufflés and soufflé omelettes must be served as soon as they are cooked. They fall within moments in cool air and, if overcooked, become shrivelled and dry.

For sabayon, whisk the mixture over even, gentle heat so that it gradually thickens to be close-textured and delicate. If cooked too long or over too high a heat, the egg yolks will grain and separate.

If it is to be served warm, sabayon can be kept for only a few minutes but, if it is beaten after cooking until cool, it can be held for an hour or two.

Coffee Souffle

SOUFFLE AU CAFE

Coffee, Grand Marnier, mocha and vanilla are a few possible flavours for this archetypal soufflé.

SERVES 4-6

8 fl oz/250 ml milk
3 egg yolks
3½ oz/100 g caster sugar
1 oz/30 g plain flour
2 tablespoons dry instant coffee, dissolved in 2 tablespoons hot water
5 egg whites
powdered sugar (for sprinkling)

2 pt/1.25 litre soufflé dish*

For soufflé base: scald milk. Meanwhile, whip* egg yolks with half the sugar until thick and light, about 2 minutes. Stir in flour. Whisk* hot milk into yolk mixture, blend well, return to the pan and whisk over gentle heat until boiling and thickened. Continue simmering 2 minutes. Take from heat and stir in dissolved coffee.

Half an hour before serving heat oven to gas 7/425°F/220°C. Generously butter the soufflé dish. Stiffly whip egg whites*, add remaining sugar and continue beating until glossy to make a meringue, about 1 minute. Heat coffee mixture until hot to the touch. Take from heat and stir in about a quarter of meringue until well mixed. Add this mixture back to remaining egg whites and fold* together as lightly as possible. Transfer mixture to soufflé dish, smooth the top, and bake until puffed and brown, 12-15 minutes. Sprinkle with powdered sugar and serve at once.

GETTING AHEAD

Coffee mixture can be kept for up to 6 hours in the refrigerator, but meringue should be added just before baking.

VARIATIONS

Grand Marnier Soufflé (Soufflé au Grand Marnier)
Add ¼ oz/ 7 g more flour. Substitute 3 tablespoons Grand Marnier and grated zest of 2 oranges for coffee.

Mocha Soufflé (Soufflé au moka)
Melt 2 oz/60 g chocolate, chopped, in the milk and use same amount coffee.

Vanilla Soufflé (Soufflé à la vanille)
Omit coffee and infuse milk with vanilla pod for 15-20 minutes or add a few drops vanilla essence to custard base.

**For more detailed information about terms marked with an asterisk, see Glossary pp. 88-91.*

EXOTIC FRUIT SOUFFLE WITH VANILLA CUSTARD SAUCE

SOUFFLE AUX FRUITS EXOTIQUES, CREME ANGLAISE

Exotic fruits are losing their claim to the name now that so many are available fresh or in jars. For this recipe fresh or bottled purée of a tart fruit like passion fruit, mango or pomegranate is best.

SERVES 8

16 fl oz/500 ml fruit purée

1 tablespoon arrowroot, mixed to a paste with 3 tablespoons water

3 oz/90 g caster sugar, more if needed

5 egg whites

powdered sugar (for sprinkling)

To serve

vanilla custard sauce *(p. 33)*

3¼ pt/2 litre soufflé dish*

In a small pan bring fruit purée just to a boil. Whisk in arrowroot paste, adding just enough to thicken the mixture to the consistency of thick cream. *Note*: all the arrowroot may not be needed. Let the mixture cool slightly, add half the sugar and taste, adding more if needed.

Half an hour before serving heat oven to gas 7/425°F/220°C. Generously butter the soufflé dish. Stiffly whip egg whites*, add remaining sugar and continue beating until glossy to make a meringue, about 1 minute.

Heat fruit mixture until hot to the touch. Take from heat and stir in about a quarter of meringue until well mixed. Add this mixture back to remaining meringue and fold* together as lightly as possible.

Transfer mixture to soufflé dish, smooth the top and bake until puffed and brown, 12-15 minutes. Sprinkle with powdered sugar and serve at once. Serve the chilled vanilla custard sauce separately.

GETTING AHEAD

Provided that the meringue is stiffly beaten, the finished soufflé can be kept for up to 2 hours in the refrigerator before baking.

VARIATIONS

Raspberry Soufflé with Liqueur Custard Sauce
(Soufflé aux framboises, crème à la liqueur de framboises)
Use fresh raspberry purée as the fruit, sieving it to remove seeds. Flavour vanilla custard sauce with 2 tablespoons raspberry liqueur.

Rhubarb Soufflé with Vanilla Custard Sauce
(Soufflé à la rhubarbe, crème anglaise)
Cook 1 lb/500 g prepared rhubarb with 4 fl oz/125 ml water and 1½ oz/45 g caster sugar. Purée cooked rhubarb thoroughly in the food processor to avoid strings.

Strawberry and Mint Souffle

SOUFFLE AUX FRAISES A LA MENTHE

Mint is good with many summer fruits.

SERVES 8

1 lb/500 g fresh strawberries, hulled
bunch of mint
8 fl oz/250 ml milk
3 egg yolks
3 oz/90g caster sugar
1 oz/30 g plain flour
2 tablespoons Kirsch
few drops lemon juice
5 egg whites
powdered sugar (for sprinkling)

3¼ pt/2 litre soufflé dish* or eight 8 fl oz/250 ml ramekins*

Purée strawberries, reserving 8 for decoration, and measure 16 fl oz/500 ml purée. Remove mint leaves from stems, reserving 4 sprigs for decoration, and chop leaves to make 2 tablespoons.

For soufflé base: scald milk. Meanwhile, whip* egg yolks with half the sugar until thick and light, about 2 minutes. Stir in flour. Whisk* hot milk into yolk mixture, blend well, return to pan and whisk over gentle heat until boiling and thickened. Add strawberry purée and continue to boil, stirring constantly, for 5 minutes. Take from heat and let cool slightly. Stir in chopped mint, Kirsch and lemon juice.

Half an hour before serving heat oven to gas 7/425°F/220°C. Generously butter the soufflé dish. Stiffly whip egg whites*, add remaining sugar and continue beating until glossy to make a meringue, about 1 minute.

Heat strawberry mixture until hot to the touch. Take from heat and stir in about a quarter of meringue until well mixed. Add this mixture back to remaining egg whites and fold* together as lightly as possible.

Transfer mixture to soufflé dish and smooth the top. Bake until puffed and brown, 8-10 minutes for a small soufflé and 15-20 minutes for a large one.

Sprinkle with powdered sugar, top soufflé with mint sprigs and strawberries (halved if large). Serve at once.

GETTING AHEAD

The strawberry mixture can be kept for up to 3 hours in the refrigerator, but the meringue should be added just before baking.

VARIATIONS

Banana Soufflé with Rum Custard Sauce
(Soufflé de banane, crème anglaise au rhum)
Omit mint and substitute 3 puréed ripe bananas for strawberries and rum for Kirsch. Serve with chilled rum custard sauce (p. 33).

Mint Julep Soufflé (Soufflé au whisky à la menthe)
Omit strawberries. Substitute 6 tablespoons bourbon for Kirsch.

Souffle Jam Omelette

OMELETTE SOUFFLEE A LA CONFITURE

Like savoury omelettes, a sweet omelette can have a great variety of flavours and fillings.

SERVES 2

3-4 tablespoons strawberry, raspberry or black cherry jam
4 eggs, separated
few drops vanilla essence
2 oz/60 g caster sugar
½ oz/15 g butter
powdered sugar (for sprinkling)

9 in/22 cm omelette pan* or non-stick frying pan
metal skewer (optional)

Heat oven to gas 5/375°F/190°C or light the grill. Melt jam and keep warm.

For omelette: whip* egg yolks and vanilla essence with half the sugar until light and very thick, about 5 minutes. Stiffly whip egg whites*, add remaining sugar and continue beating until glossy to make a meringue, about 1 minute. Stir a little meringue into egg yolk mixture, then add to remaining meringue and fold* together as lightly as possible.

Heat butter in the pan until foaming. Pour in egg mixture and cook over medium heat until omelette is puffed and brown underneath, ½-1 minute. Put pan in oven until top is browned, 3-4 minutes, or brown it under the grill.

Turn omelette on to a plate sprinkled with powdered sugar, spoon jam into centre and fold omelette in half. Sprinkle with more sugar. If you like, heat a skewer on burner and mark sugar in a lattice pattern. Serve at once.

GETTING AHEAD

A soufflé omelette only takes a few minutes to make, but it cannot be prepared ahead.

VARIATIONS

Apple Soufflé Omelette (Omelette à la Normande)
Fry 2 dessert apples, peeled, cored and sliced, in ½ oz/15 g butter and ½ oz/15 g caster sugar, tossing constantly so sugar caramelizes. When brown, stir in 2 tablespoons double cream. Make omelette and fill with hot apple filling. If liked, flame with Calvados.

Flamed Soufflé Omelette (Omelette flambée)
Make omelette and fill with jam if you like. In a small pan heat 2-3 tablespoons rum, brandy or Grand Marnier, flame and pour over omelette. Serve at once.

Chocolate Souffle

SOUFFLE AU CHOCOLAT

The richest possible chocolate soufflé, using no flour.

SERVES 4

4 oz/125 g plain chocolate, chopped
4 fl oz/125 ml strong black coffee
3 egg yolks
few drops vanilla essence
5 egg whites
1 oz/30 g caster sugar
powdered sugar (for sprinkling)

To serve

Chantilly cream, made with 4 fl oz/125 ml double cream*

1⅔ pt/1 litre soufflé dish*

In a heavy pan melt chocolate in coffee, stirring constantly. Cook until mixture is thick but still falls easily from the spoon, 2-3 minutes. Take from heat and beat in egg yolks. *Note*: the heat will cook and thicken the egg yolks. Add vanilla essence.

Half an hour before serving heat oven to gas 7/425°F/220°C. Generously butter the soufflé dish.

Stiffly whip egg whites*, add sugar and continue beating until glossy to make a meringue, about 1 minute.

Heat chocolate mixture until hot to the touch. Take from heat and stir in about a quarter of meringue until well mixed. Add this mixture back to remaining meringue and fold* together as lightly as possible.

Transfer mixture to soufflé dish, smooth the top and bake until puffed and a crust has formed on top, 12-15 minutes. Sprinkle with powdered sugar and serve at once. Serve chilled Chantilly cream separately.

GETTING AHEAD

The chocolate mixture can be kept for up to 6 hours in the refrigerator, but the meringue should be added just before baking.

VARIATIONS

Chocolate Apple Soufflé
(Soufflé au chocolat et aux pommes)
Peel, core and thinly slice 2 dessert apples. Fry in ½ oz/15 g butter until very soft. Mash to a purée and stir into chocolate mixture with vanilla.

Chocolate Hazelnut Soufflé
(Soufflé au chocolat et aux noisettes)
Finely chop 2 oz/60 g toasted* peeled hazelnuts. Stir into chocolate mixture with vanilla and 1 tablespoon brandy.

SABAYON SAUCE

SAUCE SABAYON

A sauce to serve warm or chilled.

SERVES 4

4 egg yolks
2 oz/60 g caster sugar
¼ pt/150 ml dry white wine
grated zest of 1 orange or 1 lemon

copper or stainless steel bowl* (optional)

Put egg yolks, sugar and wine in a bowl, preferably copper or stainless steel, over a pan of hot water. Whisk over hot but not boiling water until sauce is frothy and thick enough to leave a ribbon trail*, 5-8 minutes. Do not heat the sauce too much or overcook it, or it will curdle. Take from heat and whisk in zest.

If serving sauce warm, serve it at once. If serving cold, whisk until cool, then set bowl over ice and whisk sauce until chilled.

GETTING AHEAD

After chilling, sabayon sauce can be kept for up to 1 hour in the refrigerator. It cannot be reheated.

VARIATIONS

Gratin of Exotic Fruits
(Gratin de fruits exotiques)
Select 3-4 of following fruits: 2 kiwifruit, peeled and sliced; 1 small pineapple, peeled, cored and cut in chunks; 1 mango, peeled, cored and cut in chunks; 1 small papaya, seeds discarded and flesh scooped from skin; 2 oranges, peeled and sliced; 1 banana, sliced diagonally; 1 custard apple, peeled and sliced, discarding seeds.

Arrange fruit in 4 individual shallow baking dishes, coat with sabayon sauce and grill until lightly browned. Serve at once.

2

COLD MOUSSES AND SOUFFLES

Cold mousses and soufflés are among the prettiest and most festive of French desserts. Their airy texture, tenuously maintained by a delicate bond of gelatine, makes it possible to build elegant architectural structures which seem to defy gravity. The colours of apricot pink, lime green, caramel gold, all lightened with whipped eggs and cream to shades of pastel, add to their fragile charm.

Cold mousses and soufflés share the same foundation of either vanilla custard sauce, or eggs (whole or separated) beaten with sugar. Soufflés simply have more egg whites to lighten them. Whipped cream is added to both, with gelatine to hold the mixture together. There are a few exceptions, like chocolate mousse, which sets by itself without gelatine, and the richer iced desserts and bombes. Even apple snow is technically speaking a mousse.

The concept of a cold soufflé is a mild culinary joke, for of course the mixture does not rise in the oven, but is moulded with a soufflé collar so that it sets high above the rim of the soufflé dish. A soufflé is lighter than a mousse and the challenge is to top the fluffy tower with decoration, remove the collar and take it to the table without collapse. Part of the fun of cold soufflés and mousses is their decoration. Traditionally, rosettes of Chantilly cream are piped around the base or on top, with a clue to the flavour given by whole strawberries, candied citrus julienne and the like. Nowadays soufflés are more often left unadorned, with perhaps a dusting of powdered sugar or cocoa powder. Mousses are plainly moulded in ramekins, and served on individual plates in brilliant lakes of raspberry or redcurrant sauce. Decoration is a simple mint leaf or sliver of fruit, a stark and often stunning approach.

KEYS TO THE BEST COLD MOUSSES AND SOUFFLES

For cold soufflés and mousses to be as light as possible, all their components should be approximately the same consistency when folded to-

gether. Cream must be lightly, not stiffly, whipped and eggs whites should be beaten with sugar to make meringue.

For more instructions on beating egg whites, see Glossary (p. 88-91).

Once gelatine is added, a mousse or soufflé mixture needs constant stirring. Therefore cream, egg whites, puréed fruit and any other ingredients to be included should be prepared ahead.

Stir gently but thoroughly so that gelatine does not separate. It will set quite suddenly, so the remaining ingredients should be folded in quickly.

A generous amount of gelatine ensures a mixture will set firmly, but it is also unpleasantly rubbery to eat. Therefore gelatine content in these recipes has been kept to a minimum.

Don't risk a mould that is tall or elaborate, for mousses and soufflés collapse easily; a ring or Kugelhopf mould is best.

Choose tart fruit flavourings, such as raspberry or citrus, which can balance the high amounts of cream and egg white. Where acidity is low, as with peaches, add lemon juice or a spirit such as Kirsch.

Do not leave an acid fruit such as raspberry in a metal mould overnight as it will discolour.

Cold soufflés and mousses keep well, but their gelatine content stiffens on standing. If making them ahead, either leave them for 1-2 hours at room temperature to soften, or reduce gelatine content slightly to compensate.

If frozen, almost all cold mousses and soufflés will separate on thawing.

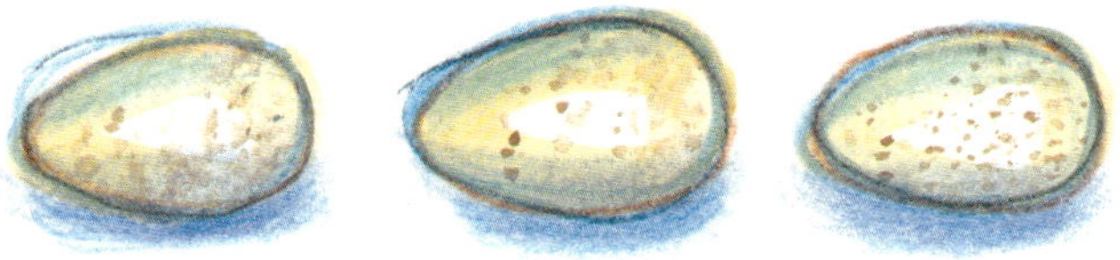

CHOCOLATE MOUSSE

MOUSSE AU CHOCOLAT

Good dessert chocolate really makes a difference.

SERVES 4

6 oz/175 g plain chocolate, chopped

2 fl oz/60 ml strong black coffee

4 eggs, separated

few drops vanilla essence or 1 tablespoon rum

2 tablespoons caster sugar

To decorate

Chantilly cream, made with 4 fl oz/125 ml double cream*

*4 chocolate discs**

4 mousse pots or stemmed glasses
pastry bag* and large star tube*

In a heavy pan melt chocolate in coffee over low heat, stirring. Cook until mixture is creamy but still falls easily from the spoon. Take from the heat, let cool slightly, then beat in egg yolks one by one. *Note*: the hot mixture will cook and thicken the egg yolks slightly. Stir in vanilla essence or rum.

Stiffly whip egg whites*, add sugar and continue beating 30 seconds. If necessary, reheat chocolate mixture until hot to the touch. Add to egg whites and fold* together as lightly as possible. Spoon mixture into the pots or glasses and chill for at least 6 hours.

To decorate: not more than 2 hours before serving, using the pastry bag, pipe* large rosettes of Chantilly cream on the top of each mousse. Decorate each with a chocolate disc. Chill until serving.

GETTING AHEAD

The flavour of chocolate mousse improves on standing; it can be kept for up to 3 days in the refrigerator.

VARIATION

Orange Chocolate Mousse
(Mousse au chocolat à l'orange)
Substitute orange juice for coffee and top Chantilly cream rosettes with candied orange julienne*.

ORANGE MOUSSE GATEAU

GATEAU A LA MOUSSE D'ORANGE

Half mousse, half cake, this is a favourite new-style dessert.

SERVES 8

For genoise
3 oz/90 g plain flour
pinch of salt
1½ oz/45 g unsalted butter
3 eggs
3 oz/90 g caster sugar
few drops vanilla essence
*4 fl oz/125 ml sugar syrup**
2 tablespoons Grand Marnier

For orange mousse
8 fl oz/250 ml orange juice
½ oz/15 g gelatine
8 fl oz/250 ml double cream
2 eggs
2 egg yolks
3 oz/90 g caster sugar
zest of 1 orange, grated
3 tablespoons Grand Marnier
10 oz/300 g orange jelly or marmalade

To decorate
*5-6 thin candied orange slices**

10 in/25 cm cake tin*
9 in/23 cm spring-form tin*

Make genoise (p. 72) and bake in the cake tin. Trim cake to fit the spring-form tin and split cake horizontally. Sprinkle the cut side of each half of cake with sugar syrup and Grand Marnier. Line spring-form tin with a round of cardboard and set a cake half on top, cut side up.

For mousse: put half orange juice in a small pan, sprinkle over gelatine* and let stand until spongy, about 5 minutes. Whip cream until it holds soft peaks and chill.

In a large bowl beat eggs, egg yolks, sugar, orange zest and remaining orange juice until mixed. Set bowl over a pan of hot but not boiling water and beat until mixture is light and holds a ribbon trail* when the whisk is lifted, 8-10 minutes. Take from heat and whisk until cool.

Melt gelatine over low heat and stir thoroughly into orange mixture with Grand Marnier. Set bowl over ice and water and chill, stirring gently, until mixture starts to thicken. At once fold* in lightly whipped cream. Pour mousse into spring-form tin and set second cake half on top, cut side down, pushing lightly to level it. Cover and chill until firm, at least 2 hours.

Melt orange jelly or marmalade and, if using marmalade, sieve it. Pour over cake to form an even glaze and leave to set.

To decorate: not more than 2 hours before serving, run a knife around sides of spring-form tin and unmould gâteau. Cut candied orange slices in half and press semicircles against the layer of mousse to form a scalloped pattern.

GETTING AHEAD

Orange mousse gâteau can be kept for up to 2 days in the refrigerator. Let it stand at room temperature for an hour to soften slightly before serving.

VARIATIONS

Lemon Mousse Gâteau
(Gâteau à la mousse au citron)
Substitute 4 fl oz/125 ml lemon juice for orange juice and omit Grand Marnier. Glaze with lemon marmalade. Decorate with candied lemon slices*.

Strawberry Mousse Gâteau
(Gâteau à la mousse de fraises)
Substitute strawberry mousse (p. 21) for orange mousse. Glaze cake with clear strawberry jam and decorate gâteau with wafer-thin slices cut from the centre of large strawberries. Omit candied orange.

Crystallized Fruit and Liqueur Souffle

SOUFFLE ROTHSCHILD

This cold version of a classic hot soufflé is flavoured with macerated crystallized fruits. The liqueur is Dantziger Goldwasser, a type of Kirsch flecked with gold leaf – hence the soufflé's name.

SERVES 8

6 tablespoons cold water

½ oz/15 g gelatine

8 fl oz/250 ml double cream

4 fl oz/125 ml Dantziger Goldwasser or Kirsch

4 oz/125 g mixed crystallized fruits, chopped very finely

For vanilla custard sauce

½ pt/300 ml milk

1 vanilla pod or few drops vanilla essence

4 egg yolks

1 oz/30 g caster sugar

4 egg whites

3½ oz/100 g caster sugar

To decorate

Chantilly cream, made with 8 fl oz/250 ml double cream*

10-12 crystallized cherries

2⅓ pt/1.5 litre soufflé dish*
pastry bag* and medium star tube*

Wrap a collar* around the soufflé dish. Put water in a small pan, sprinkle over gelatine* and leave until spongy, at least 5 minutes. Whip cream until it holds soft peaks and chill. Mix 2 tablespoons Goldwasser or Kirsch with crystallized fruits and leave to macerate.

Make vanilla custard sauce (p. 33). Melt gelatine over low heat and stir thoroughly into custard with macerated fruits. Set bowl over ice and water and chill, stirring occasionally, until mixture starts to set.

Meanwhile, stiffly whip egg whites*, add sugar and continue whisking until glossy to make a meringue about 1 minute. As soon as fruit mixture starts to set, stir in remaining Goldwasser or Kirsch. Fold* in meringue, followed by whipped cream. Work fast as mixture sets quickly. Spoon mixture into prepared soufflé dish – it should fill well above rim of the dish. Smooth the top of soufflé and chill until set, at least 6 hours.

To decorate: not more than 2 hours before serving, trim collar level with soufflé mixture. Spread a thin layer of Chantilly cream on surface of soufflé and mark a lattice pattern with the point of a knife. Using the pastry bag, pipe* rosettes of remaining Chantilly cream at edge of soufflé.

Pour boiling water over crystallized cherries to remove sugar, then drain and dry them. If large, halve them, and set on top of rosettes. Chill the soufflé. Just before serving, remove collar, easing it away from sides of soufflé with a knife. Set dish on a plate for serving.

GETTING AHEAD

Soufflé Rothschild can be kept for up to 24 hours in the refrigerator. Let it stand at room temperature for a few minutes to soften before serving.

VARIATIONS

Cold Ginger Soufflé with Whisky
(Soufflé froid au gingembre et whisky)
Replace crystallized fruits with crystallized ginger, and Goldwasser with whisky.

Cold Grand Marnier Soufflé
(Soufflé froid au Grand Marnier)
Use only crystallized orange peel and replace Goldwasser with 6 tablespoons Grand Marnier and 2 tablespoons brandy.

APRICOT MOUSSE WITH FRESH ORANGE SAUCE

MOUSSE AUX ABRICOTS, SAUCE A L'ORANGE

Canned apricots in light syrup can be used instead of fresh apricots in this recipe, which is served with a tangy orange sauce.

SERVES 10

2 lb/1 kg fresh apricots, halved, stones removed and poached, or 2 lb/1 kg canned apricots in light syrup*

½ oz/15 g gelatine

½ pt/300 ml double cream

3 eggs

2 egg yolks

5 oz/150 g caster sugar

2 tablespoons Kirsch

To decorate

fresh orange sauce (p. 22)

Chantilly cream, made with 4 fl oz/125 ml double cream*

sprigs of fresh mint (optional)

ten 6 fl oz/175 ml ramekins* or 3¼ pt/2 litre ring mould* pastry bag* and small star tube*

Drain poached or canned apricots, reserving 4 fl oz/125 ml syrup and 10 of the best apricot halves for decoration. Purée remainder in a blender or food processor. Purée should measure ¾ pt/475 ml. In a small pan, sprinkle gelatine* over reserved syrup and let stand until spongy, about 5 minutes. Whip cream until it holds soft peaks and chill.

In a large bowl, beat eggs, egg yolks and sugar until blended. If using an electric mixer*, beat at high speed until mixture is thick and light and leaves a ribbon trail*, 4-5 minutes. If you have no electric mixer, set bowl over a pan of hot but not boiling water and whisk until mixture is light and

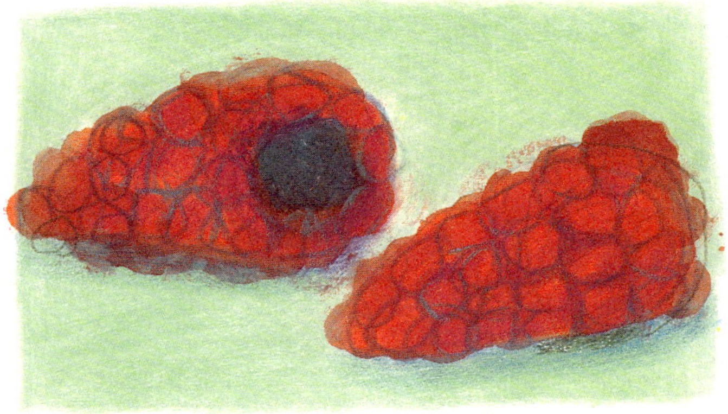

leaves a ribbon trail, then continue beating, off the heat, until mixture is cool.

Stir apricot purée into cool egg mixture. Melt gelatine over low heat and stir thoroughly into mixture. Set bowl over ice and water and chill, stirring gently, until mixture starts to thicken. At once fold* in lightly whipped cream and Kirsch. Pour mixture into the ramekins or mould. Work fast as mixture sets quickly. Cover and chill until firmly set, at least 2 hours.

To decorate: unmould mousse(s) by running a knife around edge of each ramekin or mould and dipping the bottoms in a pan of warm water for a few seconds. Turn out on to individual plates or a serving plate. Top with reserved apricot halves and spoon redcurrant sauce around the edge. Using the pastry bag, pipe* rosettes of Chantilly cream around the edge of each apricot half, adding mint sprigs if liked.

GETTING AHEAD

Apricot mousse and sauce can be kept for up to 24 hours in the refrigerator. After decorating mousse, let it stand at room temperature for a few minutes to soften before serving.

VARIATIONS

Raspberry or Strawberry Mousse
(Mousse de framboises ou fraises)
Substitute ¾ pt/475 ml fresh raspberry or strawberry purée for poached apricot purée, sieving raspberry purée to remove seeds. Decorate mousse with raspberries or strawberries, and serve vanilla custard sauce (p. 33) instead of orange sauce.

Fresh Orange Sauce

SAUCE A L'ORANGE

Good with creamy desserts and ice-cream.

MAKES ¾ pt/450 ml

3 oranges
4 tablespoons orange marmalade
4 fl oz/125 ml orange juice
4 fl oz/125 ml water
1 tablespoon Grand Marnier
caster sugar, to taste

With a vegetable peeler, remove zest of 1 orange. Cut zest in thin julienne* strips and put them in a pan of cold water. Simmer for 2 minutes, drain, rinse and drain again.

With a serrated knife, cut skin, including pith, from all 3 oranges. Cut out orange segments, discarding membranes and reserving any juice.

Melt marmalade in a saucepan, sieve it and put back in pan. Add orange juice, including any from oranges, and water. Heat, stirring gently, until sauce is smooth. Let cool, then stir in orange segments, orange julienne and Grand Marnier. Taste, adding sugar if necessary. Serve chilled.

GETTING AHEAD

Fresh orange sauce can be kept for up to 24 hours in a refrigerator.

Caramel Mousse

MOUSSE AU CARAMEL

Be sure to cook the caramel to a deep golden brown so this mousse tastes nutty and not too sweet.

SERVES 8

caramel, made with 5 oz/150 g caster sugar*
8 fl oz/250 ml cold water
½ oz/15 g gelatine
½ pt/300 ml double cream
4 eggs
3 egg yolks
4½ oz/135 g caster sugar

To decorate

Chantilly cream, made with 8 fl oz/250 ml double cream*

To serve

fresh orange sauce (p. 22)

3¼ pt/2 litre Kugelhopf or plain ring mould*
pastry bag* and medium star tube*

Make caramel*. As soon as it is dark, take from heat and add half the cold water. Stand back as caramel will splutter. Heat gently until caramel dissolves, then leave to cool. Sprinkle gelatine* over remaining cold water in a small pan and let stand until spongy, about 5 minutes. Whip cream until it holds soft peaks and chill.

In a large bowl, beat eggs, egg yolks and sugar until blended. If using an electric mixer*, beat at high speed until mixture is thick and light and leaves a ribbon trail*, 5-8 minutes. If you have no electric mixer, set bowl over a pan of hot but not boiling water and whisk until mixture is light and leaves a ribbon trail, then continue beating, off the heat, until mixture is cool.

Melt gelatine over low heat and stir thoroughly into egg mixture. Set bowl over ice and water and chill, stirring gently, until mixture starts to thicken. At once fold in cool caramel, followed by lightly whipped cream. Pour mixture into the mould. Work fast as the egg mixture sets quickly once it starts to thicken. Cover mousse and chill until firmly set, at least 6 hours.

To decorate: not more than 2 hours before serving, unmould mousse by dipping mould into a pan of lukewarm water for a few seconds and running a knife around the edges of the mould. Turn out on to a serving plate. Using the pastry bag, pipe* rosettes of Chantilly cream on top of mousse.

Chill until serving. Serve fresh orange sauce separately.

GETTING AHEAD

Caramel mousse can be kept for up to 24 hours in the refrigerator. After decorating, let it stand at room temperature for a few minutes to soften before serving.

COLD LIME SOUFFLE

SOUFFLE FROID AU CITRON VERT

The juiciness of limes varies, though 1 usually yields about 3 tablespoons juice.

SERVES 8

4 tablespoons cold water

½ oz/15 g gelatine

8 fl oz/250 ml double cream

4 eggs, separated

6½ oz/200 g caster sugar

4 fl oz/125 ml lime juice

To decorate

Chantilly cream, made with 8 fl oz/250 ml double cream*

candied julienne of 2 limes or 12-15 whole blanched* pistachios*

4 tablespoons blanched chopped pistachios*

2⅓ pt/1.5 litre soufflé dish*
pastry bag* and medium star tube*

Wrap a collar* around the soufflé dish. Put water in a small pan, sprinkle over gelatine* and leave until spongy, about 5 minutes. Whip cream until it holds soft peaks and chill.

In a large bowl beat egg yolks, two-thirds of sugar and lime juice until mixed. Set bowl over a pan of hot but not boiling water and beat until mixture is light and thick enough to hold a ribbon trail* when the whisk is lifted, 8-10 minutes. Take from the heat and whisk until cool.

Meanwhile, melt gelatine over low heat. Beat gelatine into warm lime mixture and continue beating until mixture is cool. Set bowl over ice and chill, stirring occasionally, until mixture starts to set. Stiffly whip egg whites*, add remaining sugar and continue beating until glossy to make a meringue, about 1 minute. As soon as lime mixture starts to set, fold* in meringue followed by whipped cream. Work fast as mixture sets quickly. Spoon mixture into prepared soufflé dish – it should fill well above the rim of the dish. Smooth top of soufflé and chill until set, at least 3 hours.

To decorate: not more than 2 hours before serving, trim collar level with soufflé mixture. Using the pastry bag, pipe* rosettes of Chantilly cream at edge of soufflé. Top rosettes with candied lime julienne or whole pistachios and chill the soufflé again.

Just before serving, remove collar, easing it from soufflé with a knife. Press chopped pistachios around edge and set soufflé dish on a plate for serving.

GETTING AHEAD

Lime soufflé can be kept for up to 24 hours in the refrigerator. After adding pistachios, let it stand for a few minutes at room temperature to soften before serving.

3

MOULDED CHARLOTTES & CREAMS

Creams and custards amount to so much more than the simple sum of eggs, sugar and milk. Baked caramel cream and pots de crème last far beyond the nursery, where most of us encounter them first. That other childhood standby, vanilla custard, also stars as a hot or cold sauce, forms the basis of cold soufflés and is the main ingredient, together with whipped cream and a binding of gelatine, in the Bavarian creams of French cuisine.

Vanilla, caramel, coffee and chocolate are the classic flavours for creams and custards. Alternatives abound, but they must be used with care as eggs and milk are easily overwhelmed. The grated zest of a lime, lemon or orange (juice would curdle the milk), a dash of liqueur, or a sprinkling of spice (particularly nutmeg) are all suitable for custards. Fruits like raspberry need the addition of cream, as in a bavarois, to help balance the acidity.

Bavarian creams, renowned for their melting texture, have recently taken on a fresh look. Their delicate colours are displayed to advantage by setting them in a shallow flat mould so their surface gleams like a mirror on the plate. They are now scarcely distinguishable from charlottes, which are often also set in a shallow mould, with a thin layer of sponge cake on the base or around the sides.

In the old days a charlotte could safely be identified by its characteristic bucket shape, as tall as the base was wide. The sides would be lined with ladyfingers or wafers, the height was emphasized by vertical lines of whipped cream and the top bore a froth of rosettes and sugared fruits.

Such frivolities are bound to return, if only because simplest effects are the hardest to achieve, and a little cream can hide a multitude of sins. This chapter takes a look at the whole wide field of moulded creams with some new, and some classical, ideas.

KEYS TO THE BEST MOULDED CHARLOTTES AND CREAMS

When baking or cooking an egg custard, the mixture must never reach boiling point. If heated too

fast or too long, the eggs will curdle and separate from the milk.

When baking custards, to ensure a low steady heat a water bath is always used. For custard sauce, some cooks prefer a double boiler, but I find a heavy-bottomed pan is sufficient precaution.

If a binder like flour or cornflour is added to custard it will be less rich, but the milk and egg yolk emulsion will be stabilized sufficiently for you to boil the custard without danger of curdling.

If egg whites are included in custard as well as egg yolks (this is usual when it is to be unmoulded), the custard will be firmer and less rich.

Custards and softer cream mixtures such as Bavarian creams do best in a shallow mould where there is less risk of collapse. Charlotte mixtures, particularly when set in the traditional bucket mould, must be quite firm.

Ladyfingers are often used to line and support the sides of a charlotte. Many Bavarian creams are also given sponge sides or set on a layer of sponge cake to give them body.

Whipped cream is added to a Bavarian mixture for lightness, but don't overdo it. The consistency should be smooth, without the fluffiness of a mousse.

Most moulded creams can be kept for a day or two before turning out. Those containing gelatine should be left for an hour or two at room temperature to soften slightly before serving.

Do not freeze moulded creams as they will separate.

Rich charlotte mixtures without eggs or cream can be kept in the refrigerator for a week or more, and they can also be frozen.

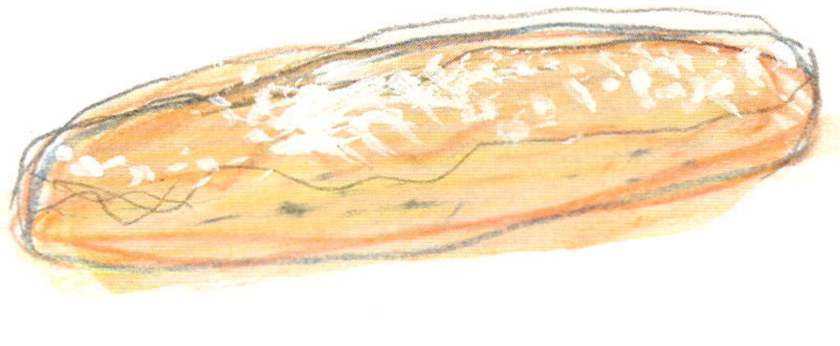

CALIFORNIAN POTS DE CREME

PETITS POTS DE CREME DE CALIFORNIE

These pots are flavoured with orange, lemon and lime, as a change from the classic coffee and chocolate. Guests are left to choose two or three.

MAKES 12 POTS – SERVES 4-6

2 oranges
3 lemons
2 limes
1⅔ pt/1 litre milk
12 egg yolks
6 oz/175 g caster sugar

To decorate

candied julienne from 1 lemon, 1 lime and ½ orange*

12 individual mousse pots with lids or 12 ramekins*

Heat oven to gas 4/350°F/180°C. Finely grate the zest from oranges, lemons and limes into 3 separate bowls. Scald milk.

Meanwhile, whip* egg yolks and sugar until light and thick, 3-5 minutes. Stir in scalded milk. Pour mixture in 3 equal portions over citrus zests. Leave to infuse 10-15 minutes.

Strain orange mixture through a fine sieve into 4 pots or ramekins. Do the same with lemon and lime mixtures. Add lids to pots or cover ramekins with foil and set them in a water bath*. Bring to the boil on top of the stove then cook in oven until custards are almost set and a knife inserted in the centre comes out clean, 20-25 minutes.

Note: do not overcook, or custards will curdle. Let them cool.

To decorate: top each pot with a pinch of appropriate candied julienne so that flavours can be identified. Serve pots at room temperature.

GETTING AHEAD

Pots de crème can be kept for up to 2 days in the refrigerator, tightly covered.

VARIATIONS

Classic Pots de Crème (Pots de crème classiques)
Scald milk with 1 vanilla pod, cover and leave to infuse, 10-15 minutes. Stir hot milk into egg mixture, reserving vanilla pod, and divide custard mixture into 3 portions. Leave one portion flavoured with vanilla. Stir 2 teaspoons dry instant coffee into the second portion, and 3 oz/90 g plain chocolate, chopped and melted on a heatproof plate over hot water, into the third. Strain custard mixtures into pots and cook.
Oriental Pots de Crème (Pots de crème orientales)
Scald milk with 1 vanilla pod, cover and leave to infuse, 10-15 minutes. Stir hot milk into egg mixture, reserving vanilla pod, and divide custard into 3 portions. Stir ½ teaspoon grated nutmeg into one portion, 1 teaspoon orange flower water or rose water into the second portion, and ¼ teaspoon ground cardamom into the third. Strain custard mixtures into pots and cook.

CARAMEL CREAM

CREME CARAMEL

Caramel cream can be baked in individual dishes or one large one.

SERVES 4

For caramel	*2 eggs*
3¼ oz/100 g caster sugar	*2 egg yolks*
	2 oz/60 g caster sugar
¾ pt/450 ml milk	*few drops vanilla essence*

1⅔ pt/1 litre soufflé dish* or 4 ramekins*

Heat oven to gas 4/350°F/180°C. Make caramel (p. 88) and let bubbles subside. Pour into ramekins or soufflé dish and turn at once so the sides and base are coated. Let caramel cool and set.

Scald milk and let cool slightly. Whip* eggs and egg yolks with sugar until thoroughly mixed, then whisk in milk. Stir in vanilla essence. Strain custard into the lined ramekins or soufflé dish and set in a water bath*.

Bring water bath to the boil on top of stove, then cook in oven until creams are almost set and a knife inserted in the centre comes out clean, 20-25 minutes for small creams and 40-50 minutes for a large one. *Note*: do not overcook or creams will curdle. Let them cool completely in the ramekins or dish.

To unmould creams: shortly before serving, run a knife around edge of ramekins or dish and turn creams on to individual plates or a deep serving dish (the caramel will have dissolved to form a sauce). Serve at room temperature.

GETTING AHEAD

Caramel cream can be cooked up to 48 hours ahead and kept in the refrigerator, tightly covered. Turn it out not more than 15 minutes before serving as the caramel discolours on standing.

VARIATIONS

Baked Custard (Flan à la muscade)
Omit caramel lining and mix 1 teaspoon grated nutmeg into custard before baking in individual dishes. Serve in the dishes.
Chestnut Caramel Cream
(Crème caramel aux marrons)
After lining dishes with caramel, sprinkle on top 8 oz/250 g crumbled commercial candied chestnuts (marrons glacés). Flavour custard mixture with 2 tablespoons rum. Turn out to serve.

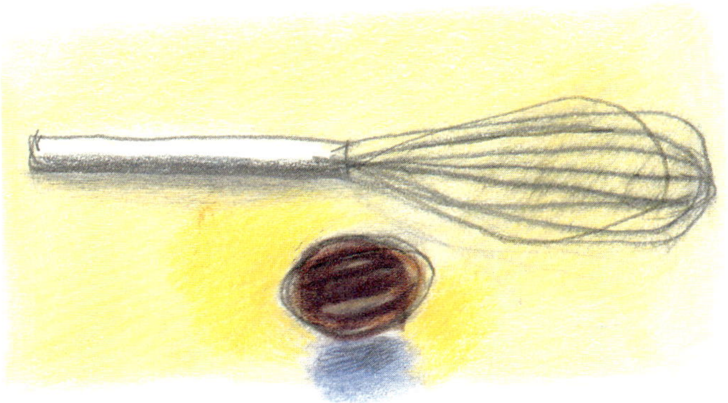

Striped Bavarian Cream

BAVAROIS RUBANE

The taller the peaks of the mould, the more dramatic the striped layers of this cream appear.

SERVES 6-8

8 fl oz/250 ml double cream

For vanilla custard sauce

1 pt/600 ml milk

1 vanilla pod

8 egg yolks

2 oz/60 g caster sugar

*½ oz/15 g gelatine**

4 tablespoons water

1½ oz/45 g plain chocolate, chopped

2 teaspoons dry instant coffee, dissolved in 2 teaspoons hot water

To serve

cold chocolate sauce (p. 32)

---

2 pt/1.25 litre peaked mould* or fluted ring mould*

Whip the cream until it holds a soft peak. Make vanilla custard sauce (p. 33). Sprinkle gelatine* over water in a small pan and leave until spongy, about 5 minutes. Melt gelatine over low heat and stir into custard sauce while still warm. Divide custard equally into 3 bowls.

Melt chocolate on a heatproof plate over a pan of hot water and stir into one portion of custard. Stir dissolved coffee into another portion and set bowl over ice and water. Chill, stirring, until mixture starts to set. Fold* in about a third of whipped cream and pour mixture into the mould. Work fast as mixture sets quickly. Chill until set, 10-15 minutes.

Chill vanilla mixture, fold in half the remaining cream and leave to set also. Finally chill chocolate custard, fold in remaining cream and pour into mould. Chill until very firm, at least 6 hours.

To serve: just before serving, dip mould for 5-10 seconds in warm water. Pull mixture away from rim with your fingertips to break the airlock, and unmould cream on to a serving dish. Spoon a little chocolate sauce around the edge and serve the rest separately.

GETTING AHEAD

Striped Bavarian cream can be kept for up to 24 hours in the refrigerator. Let the cream stand at room temperature for 30 minutes to soften, and unmould it just before serving.

VARIATION

Striped Bavarian Cream II (Bavarois rubané II)
Omit coffee and substitute caramel* made with 1½ oz/45 g caster sugar. Dissolve caramel with 2 tablespoons water before adding to custard.

Raspberry Bavarian Cream

BAVAROIS AUX FRAMBOISES

Do not leave this dessert to stand for more than a few hours in an aluminium mould, as it will discolour because of the acidity of the raspberries.

SERVES 8-10

12 oz/375 g fresh raspberries

2 tablespoons Kirsch

3 oz/90 g caster sugar, or to taste

6 fl oz/175 ml double cream

$\frac{1}{2}$ oz/15 g gelatine

4 tablespoons water

For vanilla custard sauce

$1\frac{2}{3}$ pt/1 litre milk

1 vanilla pod

10 egg yolks

3 oz/90 g caster sugar

To decorate

mint leaves

8 in/20 cm (2 pt/1.2 litre) sloping-sided cake tin*

Reserve a dozen of the best raspberries for decoration. Purée the rest in a food processor or blender and strain to remove seeds. The purée should measure 12 fl oz/350 ml. Stir in half the Kirsch with sugar to taste. Whip cream until it holds a soft peak. In a small pan, sprinkle gelatine* over water and leave until spongy, about 5 minutes.

Make vanilla custard sauce (p. 33) and divide into 2 portions. Flavour one portion with remaining Kirsch and chill to serve as a sauce. Melt gelatine over low heat and stir into remaining portion of warm custard. Stir in raspberry purée and set bowl over ice and water. Stir until mixture starts to set.

At once take from ice and fold* in whipped cream. Pour mixture into the cake tin and chill until set, for at least 6 hours.

To decorate: not more than an hour before serving, dip tin in warm water, 10-15 seconds. With your fingertips pull edge of mixture away from mould to break airlock and turn cream out on to a serving dish. Arrange reserved raspberries with mint leaves on top in a free-form garland. Spoon a little chilled Kirsch custard around edge of cream and serve the rest separately.

GETTING AHEAD

Raspberry Bavarian cream can be kept for up to 24 hours in the refrigerator. Let it stand at room temperature for half an hour to soften, and unmould just before serving.

VARIATION

Wild Strawberry Bavarian Cream
(Bavarois aux fraises des bois)
Substitute wild strawberries for raspberries.

Chocolate and Chestnut Charlotte

CHARLOTTE AU CHOCOLAT ET AUX MARRONS

Canned chestnuts can be used instead of fresh chestnuts, but the result will not be quite so light.

SERVES 6-8

For ladyfingers

3 oz/90 g plain flour

pinch of salt

4 eggs

3¼ oz/100 g caster sugar

2 lb/1 kg fresh chestnuts or 1½ lb/750 g unsweetened canned chestnuts in water

5-6 tablespoons rum

8 oz/250 g plain chocolate, chopped

6 fl oz/175 ml water

6 oz/180 g unsalted butter

6½ oz/200 g caster sugar

To decorate

Chantilly cream, made with 4 fl oz/125 ml double cream*

chocolate discs, or 1 tablespoon grated chocolate*

To serve

pistachio or rum custard sauce (p. 33)

3¼ pt/2 litre charlotte mould*
pastry bag* and small star tube*

Make ladyfingers (p. 32). If using fresh chestnuts, peel and cook* them. Drain cooked or canned chestnuts and purée* them.

Butter the charlotte mould, line base with a round of greaseproof paper and butter it also. Put ladyfingers upright to line sides of mould, trimming them so that they fit tightly. Sprinkle 2-3 tablespoons rum on remaining ladyfingers.

Melt chocolate in water over low heat and cook, stirring, until thick and creamy. Let cool. Cream butter, add sugar and beat until light and soft, about 5 minutes. Stir in cool chocolate, remaining rum and chestnut purée. *Note*: if chocolate is warm it will melt the butter.

Spoon mixture into charlotte mould, layering it with soaked ladyfingers and ending with chocolate mixture. Smooth the top, cover with paper and chill until set, at least 6 hours.

To decorate: trim ladyfingers level with surface of mixture, unmould charlotte on to a serving plate and remove paper. Using the pastry bag, pipe* rosettes of Chantilly cream to cover the top of the charlotte. Add chocolate discs or sprinkle with grated chocolate. Spoon a little pistachio or rum custard sauce around edge of charlotte and serve the rest separately.

GETTING AHEAD

Chocolate and chestnut charlotte can be kept for up to a week in the refrigerator or frozen for up to 2 months.

VARIATION

Chocolate and Almond Charlotte
(Charlotte au chocolat et aux amandes)
Substitute 5 oz/150 g ground almonds for chestnuts and fold 4 fl oz/125 ml double cream, whipped until it holds a soft shape, into chocolate with the almonds.

Small Charlottes Malakoff with Crystallized Orange

PETITES CHARLOTTES MALAKOFF A L'ORANGE CONFITE

A layer of genoise takes the place of ladyfingers in moulding these classic little charlottes.

SERVES 10

For genoise

3 oz/90 g plain flour

pinch of salt

1½ oz/45 g unsalted butter

3 eggs

3 oz/90 g caster sugar

few drops vanilla essence

For filling

6½ oz/200 g crystallized orange peel, chopped finely

6 fl oz/175 ml Cointreau

8 oz/250 g unsalted butter

8 oz/250 g caster sugar

8 oz/250 g ground almonds

8 fl oz/250 ml double cream

To decorate

Chantilly cream, made with 4 fl oz/125 ml double cream*

5 thin slices fresh orange

To serve

fresh orange sauce (p. 22)

ten 6 fl oz/175 ml ramekins*
pastry bag* and medium star tube*

Make genoise (p. 72), spread mixture on a baking sheet lined with greaseproof paper and bake as for chocolate roulade (p. 75). With a small knife, cut out 10 rounds the diameter of the ramekins.

Butter ramekins and line bases with rounds of greaseproof paper. Mix crystallized orange peel with three-quarters of Cointreau and leave to macerate.

Cream butter, gradually beat in sugar and continue beating until soft and light, about 5 minutes. Stir in ground almonds with macerated crystallized orange peel. *Note*: do not beat or oil will be drawn out of almonds. Whip cream until it holds a soft peak and fold into almond mixture.

Fill ramekins with mixture almost to the rim. Top each with a round of genoise and sprinkle with remaining Cointreau. Cover with a sheet of greaseproof paper and chill until firmly set, at least 6 hours.

To decorate: not more than 2 hours before serving, run a knife around edge of charlottes and unmould on to individual plates, discarding paper. Using the pastry bag, pipe* a rosette of Chantilly cream on top of each charlotte. Cut orange slices in half, twist and set on the rosettes.

To serve: spoon orange sauce around the edge. Keep charlottes in the refrigerator until serving.

GETTING AHEAD

Small charlottes Malakoff can be kept for up to a week in the refrigerator, or frozen for up to 2 months. Unmould them and decorate shortly before serving.

VARIATION

Charlotte Malakoff with Strawberries
(Charlotte Malakoff aux fraises)
Substitute 8 oz/250 g sliced strawberries for crystallized orange peel, and use 4-5 tablespoons Kirsch instead of Cointreau. Decorate with whole strawberries and serve with strawberry coulis (p. 51) or raspberry sauce (p. 50).

CHOCOLATE SAUCE

SAUCE CHOCOLATE

The consistency of chocolate sauce can be varied by simmering it for a longer or shorter time.

MAKES 12 fl oz/350 ml

5 oz/150 g plain chocolate, chopped
1 oz/30 g unsalted butter
8 fl oz/250 ml water
few drops vanilla essence or 1 tablespoon brandy or rum

Melt chocolate and butter in water over a very low heat, stirring. Bring to the boil and simmer to the consistency wanted, 2-3 minutes. Let cool slightly, then stir in vanilla essence, brandy or rum. Serve hot or cold.

GETTING AHEAD

Chocolate sauce can be kept for up to a week in the refrigerator, tightly covered. Warm it slightly before serving and stir in a little water if too thick.

LADYFINGERS

BISCUITS A LA CUILLER

Ladyfingers are used to line charlotte moulds and are often served on their own with sorbet. Tricky to make, the batter must be very lightly folded so that it remains stiff enough to pipe.

MAKES ABOUT 40

3¼ oz/100 g plain flour
pinch of salt
3¼ oz/100 g caster sugar
4 eggs, separated
few drops vanilla essence
powdered sugar (for sprinkling)

pastry bag* and ¾ in/2 cm plain tube*

Butter 2 baking sheets and sprinkle with flour, shaking off the excess. Heat oven to gas 4/350°F/180°C. Sift flour and salt together twice.

Beat egg yolks with half the sugar until light and thick, 5-7 minutes. Stir in vanilla essence. Stiffly whip egg whites*, add remaining sugar and continue beating until glossy to make a meringue, about 1 minute. Sift flour over egg yolk mixture, add a quarter of the meringue and fold* together. Add remaining meringue and fold as lightly as possible.

Gently spoon mixture into the pastry bag and pipe* fingers about 4½ in/11 cm long on to baking sheets. Sprinkle powdered sugar lightly on ladyfingers. Bake until light beige and firm on outside but still soft in the centre, 15-18 minutes. *Note*: ladyfingers dry better if oven door is propped open slightly with a wooden spoon.

GETTING AHEAD

Ladyfingers are best eaten on their own the day they are baked. However, for lining a mould they should be drier and can be kept for up to 3 days in an airtight container.

VANILLA CUSTARD SAUCE

CREME ANGLAISE

Equally good hot or cold.

MAKES ½ pt/300 ml

½ pt/300 ml milk	*4 egg yolks*
1 vanilla pod or few drops vanilla essence	*1 oz/30 g caster sugar*

Bring milk just to the boil. If using vanilla pod add it, cover pan and leave over low heat to infuse, 10-15 minutes.

Meanwhile, whisk egg yolks and sugar until thick and light, about 2 minutes. Strain milk, reserving vanilla pod to use again. Stir milk into egg yolk mixture. Return custard to pan and heat gently, stirring constantly with a wooden spoon, until custard thickens slightly. A finger drawn across the back of the spoon will leave a clear trail. *Note*: do not boil or the custard will curdle.

At once take custard from the heat and strain into a cold bowl. Stir in vanilla essence if using. Serve hot or chilled.

GETTING AHEAD

Vanilla custard sauce can be kept for 2 days in the refrigerator, tightly covered.

VARIATIONS

Chocolate Custard Sauce
(Crème Anglaise au chocolat)
Add 1½ oz/45 g plain chocolate, chopped, to milk and heat until melted.

Coffee Custard Sauce (Crème anglaise au café)
While sauce is still hot, stir in 2 teaspoons dry instant coffee.

Orange Custard Sauce (Crème anglaise à l'orange)
Omit vanilla. After straining, stir grated zest of 1 orange into sauce, with 1 tablespoon Grand Marnier, if liked.

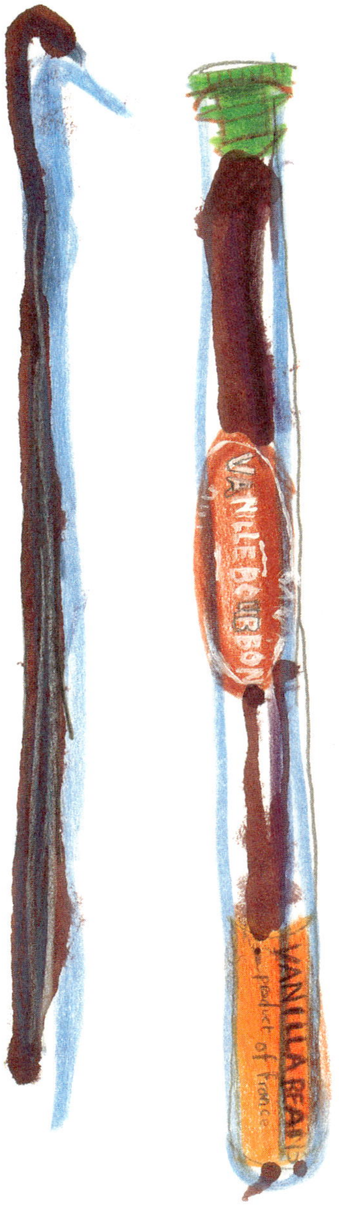

Pistachio Custard Sauce
(Crème anglaise aux pistaches)
Add 3½ oz/100 g blanched* ground pistachios to milk, cover and let infuse, 15-20 minutes. Strain out pistachios, pressing to extract all juices, and proceed with recipe.

Rum Custard Sauce (Crème anglaise au rhum)
When sauce is cold, stir in 2 tablespoons rum.

4
ICE-CREAMS AND ICED DESSERTS

Charmer of children, tempter of the most exigent gourmet, where would we be without ice-cream? The foundation is so simple – usually a base of egg custard, cream and any flavouring you like to think of, from absinthe and apricot to vanilla or watermelon.

For soufflés, mousses and other iced desserts, the mixture is even richer. Parfaits, for instance, consist of egg yolk mousse and whipped cream, usually with a flavouring like chocolate, coffee or praline. These rich mixtures have one great advantage: they can be moulded and put in the freezer without further ado.

Ice-creams, however, have a higher water content and must be stirred as they chill to smooth them and prevent the formation of ice crystals. When I was young, we used a crank-handled churn surrounded by ice and salt in a wooden bucket, which was both messy and laborious. Now cooks can choose from a professional automatic free-standing machine, a domestic model which fits in the freezer, or a modest low temperature canister which is chilled and then cranked by hand. The best home-made ice-cream is available to all.

The ice-cream itself is just the beginning. Toppings can include grated chocolate, chopped nuts, a spoonful of liqueur, or sliced fruits and whipped cream. No recipes are needed for favourites like peach Melba (vanilla ice-cream, poached peach, fresh raspberry sauce) or poire Belle Hélène (vanilla ice-cream, poached pear, hot chocolate sauce), or coupe Jacques (vanilla ice-cream and fresh fruit salad).

The hot/iced theme of baked Alaska still captures the imagination, as do iced soufflés, moulded with a paper collar, or parfaits topped with a froth of cream. Such fantasies are very Belle Epoque, an indulgence of the naughtiest 1890s kind.

KEYS TO THE BEST ICE-CREAMS AND ICED DESSERTS

Always taste an ice-cream mixture before freezing it. The flavour must be intense because it is diminished by the cold.

A squeeze of lemon juice or a touch of alcohol picks up the taste of many ice-cream mixtures. Chopped chocolate or toasted nuts add crunch.

When making parfaits and other iced desserts, meringue may be used instead of an egg yolk mousse so the mixture is lighter.

For serving, ice-cream may be moulded to turn out – a square or cone is traditional – or scooped to serve in individual bowls. Iced soufflés should be moulded with a paper collar so that the mixture rises above the rim of the dish. Parfaits are usually frozen and served in individual glasses.

The richer the mixture, the longer the ice-cream can be stored without deterioration in the freezer. Plain ice-cream can be kept for up to a month, and soufflés and parfaits for up to 3 months.

For all ice-cream desserts, ladyfingers (p. 32) or petits fours are a welcome accompaniment.

VANILLA ICE-CREAM

GLACE A LA VANILLE

A vanilla pod is essential for flavouring the best ice-cream.

MAKES 1⅔ pt/1 litre – SERVES 6

¾ pt/475 ml milk
1 vanilla pod, split
5 egg yolks
4½ oz/135 g caster sugar
8 fl oz/250 ml double cream

ice-cream machine* or churn

In a heavy pan, scald milk with vanilla pod. Cover and leave over low heat to infuse, 10-15 minutes. Meanwhile, whip* egg yolks and sugar until thick and light, about 2 minutes. Stir milk into egg yolk mixture. Return custard to the pan and heat gently, stirring constantly with a wooden spoon, until custard thickens slightly and a finger drawn across the back of the spoon leaves a clear trail. *Note*: do not boil or the custard will curdle. Remove from the heat at once and strain into a cold bowl; reserve vanilla pod to use again.

Chill custard over ice and water or in the refrigerator, then freeze in an ice-cream machine or churn until slushy. Whip cream until it holds a soft shape, then add to custard and continue churning until firm. Transfer ice-cream to a chilled mould or bowl and freeze for at least 6 hours.

To serve: to unmould ice-cream, dip the mould for 10 seconds in tepid water, run a knife around the edge and turn out on to a folded napkin on a serving dish. Alternatively, shape balls of ice-cream with a scoop and pile in individual bowls.

GETTING AHEAD

Vanilla ice-cream can be frozen for up to a month. Move it to the refrigerator for 1-2 hours to soften before serving.

VARIATIONS

Caramel Ice-Cream (Glace au caramel)
Make caramel* with 3½ oz/100 g caster sugar. Let caramel cool slightly, add milk and heat gently until all caramel is dissolved. Make the custard.

Chocolate Ice-Cream (Glace au chocolat)
Omit vanilla. Melt 8 oz/250 g plain chocolate, chopped, on a plate over hot water and stir into vanilla custard while still hot.

Coffee Ice-Cream (Glace au café)
Omit vanilla. Stir 3 tablespoons dry instant coffee into custard while still hot and stir until dissolved.

Pistachio Ice-Cream (Glace aux pistaches)
Omit vanilla. Work 3¼ oz/100 g blanched* pistachios in a blender with 2-3 tablespoons double cream to a smooth paste. Scald milk with paste, cover and infuse for 15-20 minutes. Strain before making custard, pressing out all juices.

Praline Ice-Cream (Glace au pralin)
After straining vanilla custard, stir in praline* made with 6 oz/180 g whole unblanched almonds.

Baked Alaska

OMELETTE EN SURPRISE

Baked Alaska can be lightened by adding fruit or fruit ice-cream.

SERVES 6

For genoise

3 oz/90 g plain flour

pinch of salt

1½ oz/45 g unsalted butter

2 eggs

3 oz/90 g caster sugar

For pistachio ice-cream

16 fl oz/475 ml milk

1 vanilla pod

5 egg yolks

4½ oz/135 g caster sugar

8 fl oz/250 ml double cream

3¼ oz/100 g blanched pistachios*

*2 tablespoons sugar syrup**

2 tablespoons Kirsch, rum or more sugar syrup

For Swiss meringue

6 egg whites

12 oz/375 g caster sugar

few drops vanilla essence

powdered sugar (for sprinkling)

two 8 in/20 cm square cake tins*
pastry bag* and large star tube*

Make genoise (p. 72) and bake in one of the cake tins. Remove and cool. Make pistachio ice-cream (p. 36) and freeze in the other cake tin.

Split genoise horizontally and cut each square in half. Put the two halves lengthways on a lightly buttered heatproof serving dish. Sprinkle the cut side of all four pieces of cake with sugar syrup and rum or Kirsch. Dip ice-cream tin in tepid water for 10 seconds, run a knife around the edge and turn it out. Cut in half and set the two pieces lengthways on the genoise. Cover ice-cream with remaining cake and keep in freezer.

Make Swiss meringue (p. 83). With a metal spatula spread half the meringue over ice-cream and cake. *Note*: cover them completely so that heat cannot penetrate to the ice-cream. Put remaining meringue into the pastry bag and pipe* rosettes and scrolls over the meringue. Keep in freezer.

Shortly before serving: heat oven to gas 7/ 425°F/220°C. Sprinkle meringue with powdered sugar, let stand 1 minute, then bake dessert until lightly browned, 3-5 minutes. Serve at once, cutting in thick slices like a loaf.

GETTING AHEAD

Ice-cream and cake can be frozen for up to a week. Meringue can be added 2 hours before serving and frozen also.

VARIATIONS

Baked Alaska with Fruit
(Omelette en surprise aux fruits)
Macerate 1 lb/500 g sliced strawberries in 3 tablespoons Kirsch and caster sugar to taste. Substitute strawberry ice-cream (p. 38) for pistachio ice-cream. Spread half the strawberries on the bottom layer of genoise, top with ice-cream, and spread remaining strawberries on top of ice-cream before adding second layer of genoise.

Individual Baked Alaska
(Petites omelettes en surprise)
Cut six 3 in/7 cm rounds from the genoise. Set a large scoop of ice-cream on top and coat completely with meringue rosettes. Serve on individual plates.

Peach Ice-Cream

GLACE AUX PECHES

The flavour of peaches will be enhanced by adding 1-2 drops (no more) of almond essence.

MAKES 1⅔ pt/1 litre – SERVES 6

2 oz/60 g caster sugar
4 tablespoons water
2 egg yolks
½ pt/300 ml single cream
1½ lb/750 g peaches
juice of 1 lemon
2 tablespoons Kirsch

ice-cream machine* or churn

In a small heavy pan heat sugar with water until dissolved, then boil until sugar syrup* reaches soft-ball stage, 239°F/115°C on a sugar thermometer. Let bubbles subside.

Meanwhile, in a medium bowl beat egg yolks just until mixed. Gradually pour in hot syrup, beating constantly. *Note*: if using an electric beater, pour syrup in a thin stream between beaters so syrup does not stick to bowl. Beat as fast as possible until mixture is thick and cool. Stir in cream.

Bring a large pan of water to the boil, immerse half the peaches for 10 seconds, drain and cut in half, twisting to loosen the stones. Peel them and repeat with remaining peaches. Purée peaches in a blender or food processor with lemon juice and Kirsch; it should measure ¾ pt/475 ml. Stir into egg yolk mixture. Work fast so that peaches do not discolour. Chill mixture over ice or in refrigerator until cold.

Freeze in the machine or churn until stiff. Transfer ice-cream to a chilled mould or bowl and freeze for at least 6 hours.

To serve: to unmould ice-cream, dip the mould for 10 seconds in tepid water, run a knife around the edge and turn out on to a folded napkin on a serving dish. Alternatively, shape balls of ice-cream with a scoop and pile in individual bowls.

GETTING AHEAD

Peach ice-cream can be frozen for up to 1 month. Move it to the refrigerator for an hour to soften before serving.

VARIATIONS

Mango Ice-Cream (Glace aux mangues)
Substitute 2 lb/1 kg mangoes, peeled and stones discarded, for peaches. Substitute rum for Kirsch.
Strawberry or Raspberry Ice-Cream
(Glace aux fraises ou aux framboises)
Substitute 1 lb/500 g strawberries or raspberries for peaches, and strain purée if using raspberries to remove seeds.

Coffee Parfait

PARFAIT AU CAFE

The first parfait or "perfect" iced dessert was flavoured with coffee, and it remains the most popular.

SERVES 4

3 oz/90 g caster sugar
6 tablespoons water
3 egg yolks
8 fl oz/250 ml double cream
3 tablespoons dry instant coffee, dissolved in 3 tablespoons hot water

To decorate
Chantilly cream, made with 4 fl oz/125 ml double cream*
4 chocolate discs or candied violets*

4 parfait glasses or individual freezer-proof dishes
pastry bag* and large star tube*

In a small heavy saucepan heat sugar with water until dissolved, then boil until sugar syrup* reaches soft-ball stage, 239°F/115°C on a sugar thermometer. Let bubbles subside.

Meanwhile, in a medium bowl beat egg yolks just until mixed. Gradually pour in hot syrup, beating constantly. *Note*: if using an electric beater, pour syrup in a thin stream between beaters so syrup does not stick to bowl. Beat as fast as possible until mixture is thick and cool. Whip cream until it holds a soft peak.

Beat dissolved coffee into yolk mixture. Fold* in cream. *Note*: if egg mixture is warm it will melt cream. Spoon mixture into the parfait glasses or individual freezer-proof dishes. Freeze for at least 6 hours.

To decorate: using the pastry bag, pipe* large rosettes of Chantilly cream on top of parfaits. Decorate each one with a chocolate disc or candied violet. Move them to the refrigerator for 1-2 hours to soften before serving.

GETTING AHEAD

Coffee parfaits can be frozen for up to 3 months, tightly wrapped.

VARIATIONS

Whisky Parfait (Parfait au whisky)

Substitute 5 tablespoons whisky for coffee.

Praline Parfait (Parfait au pralin)

For the coffee, substitute praline* made with 2 oz/60 g whole unblanched almonds. Top cream rosettes with toasted* blanched* almonds.

Rum Raisin Parfait

(Parfait aux raisins secs et au rhum)

Omit coffee. Soak 2½ oz/75 g dark raisins overnight in 6-7 tablespoons rum. Fold raisins and rum into egg yolk mixture, followed by cream.

Strawberry, Raspberry and Praline Bombe

(Bombe Cardinale)

Line a 2⅓ pt/1.5 litre bombe mould* with sorbet made with equal quantities of strawberries and raspberries (see raspberry sorbet p. 44). Fill with praline parfait (see above) and freeze. When unmoulded, decorate base of bombe with a ruff of Chantilly cream and serve with raspberry sauce (p. 50).

ICED STRAWBERRY SOUFFLE

SOUFFLE GLACE AUX FRAISES

A layer of ladyfingers soaked in Kirsch would make a lively surprise in these little fruit soufflés.

SERVES 10

1 lb/500 g strawberries
2 tablespoons Kirsch

For Italian meringue
8 oz/250 g caster sugar
4 fl oz/125 ml water
4 egg whites
few drops vanilla essence

½ pt/300 ml double cream

3¼ pt/2 litre soufflé dish* or
ten 6 fl oz/175 ml ramekins*

Wrap a collar* around the soufflé dish or ramekins. Chill in the freezer. Reserve 6 whole strawberries for decoration and hull the rest, washing only if they are very sandy. Purée them with Kirsch in a blender or food processor and strain to remove seeds. Make Italian meringue (p. 82) and beat until cool. Whip cream until it holds soft peaks. Fold* fruit purée into meringue, then fold in whipped cream. *Note*: if meringue is still warm it will melt cream. Spoon mixture into prepared dishes, cover and freeze at least 6 hours. To finish: halve reserved strawberries, leaving hull, and set on soufflés. Transfer to refrigerator for 1-2 hours to soften before serving.

GETTING AHEAD

Iced strawberry soufflé can be frozen for up to 3 months, tightly wrapped.

VARIATIONS

Iced Grand Marnier Soufflé

Substitute 4 fl oz/125 ml Grand Marnier, 4 tablespoons orange juice and 2 tablespoons grated orange zest for strawberry purée. Decorate with candied orange slices*.

5

SORBETS

Sorbet or sherbet comes from *charabe* the Arab word for drink. The first sorbets were indeed summer drinks made by sweetening fruit juice with sugar (a medieval Arab monopoly) and mixing it with mountain snow. Apricots, grapes, melons, pomegranates and bitter oranges were all at the disposal of the Moorish court.

The composition of sorbets has changed hardly at all and juice is still the most popular base, particularly from acid fruits like citrus. Fruit purées (fresh or cooked, depending on the type of fruit) give a slightly thicker sorbet and sweet or fizzy wines a lighter one. Mild flavours such as apple or pear are usually reinforced with an appropriate alcohol, and the 18th century habit of spicing sorbets with cinnamon or nutmeg, or perfuming them with herbs, has recently reappeared.

For a smooth texture, a sorbet must be churned constantly until firm and an ice-cream machine or churn is essential. However, a coarse-textured version called granité can be made in the freezer by whisking often as the mixture chills until it solidifies to coarse snow.

Sorbets and granités are normally scooped into stemmed glasses but lately "nouvelle" cooks have taken to shaping sorbets into egg-like ovals using 2 tablespoons dipped in water – a knack it is quite easy to acquire. The ovals are arranged, points inwards, on a chilled plate, which may be lined with a colourful fruit sauce or decorated with fruit slices and sprigs of mint.

Such dressing up is appropriate when sorbets are served as dessert, but now they also appear mid-meal, served simply in a glass as a frozen version of the *trou Normand* to clean the palate. In this role, a sorbet must be assertive, sharp with spirit not soft with sugar, and recipes must be adjusted accordingly.

KEYS TO THE BEST SORBETS

A spoonful or two of lemon juice or spirit will highlight a sorbet taste.

Tasting the ice-cold mixture just before freezing is important, for cold diminishes flavour and often extra sugar or spirit may be needed. Do not, however, be too lavish as sugar and alcohol lower the freezing point of a mixture, making it hard to set.

For lightness, many cooks add whipped egg white

MOËT & CHAN
CHAMPAGNE

when a sorbet reaches the slush stage; 1-2 teaspoons egg white is enough. The finished texture will be lighter, but less fine-grained.

Sorbets and granités set quickly but they also melt fast, so moulds and equipment used for them should always be chilled.

Sorbets can be kept for a week or two but their texture coarsens and they deteriorate more rapidly than ice-cream. After being stored, they should be left for about an hour in the refrigerator to soften before serving.

Granité should be served within 2-3 hours. Alternatively, it can be left until quite hard in the freezer and then churned for a few seconds in a food processor just before serving.

When serving a sorbet or granité, a spoonful or two of liqueur or wine on top is often welcome, together with a plate of petits fours.

Sauternes Sorbet

SORBET AU SAUTERNES

The richer and sweeter the wine, the better the sorbet will be.

MAKES 2 pt/1.2 litres – SERVES 6

3 1/4 oz/100 g caster sugar, more if needed
8 fl oz/250 ml water
juice of 2 lemons
juice of 2 oranges
1 bottle Sauternes
1 egg white

To serve

1/2 bottle Sauternes
petits fours

ice-cream machine* or churn

In a saucepan heat sugar with water over a low heat until dissolved. Boil 3 minutes and let cool. Stir in lemon and orange juice and chill mixture over ice and water or in refrigerator until very cold. Chill Sauternes.

Stir Sauternes into fruit juice mixture and taste, adding sugar if needed. Freeze the mixture in the ice-cream machine or churn, churning constantly until slushy. Beat egg white until frothy and add to mixture. Continue churning until the sorbet is firm. Pack into a chilled container, cover and freeze. To serve: scoop sorbet into stemmed glasses and set the glasses on plates. At table, pour a little Sauternes over each serving. Pass petits fours.

GETTING AHEAD

Sauternes sorbet can be kept for up to 2 weeks and should be frozen for at least 6 hours so that the flavour mellows. If frozen for more than 24 hours, move it to the refrigerator for an hour to soften before serving.

VARIATION

Champagne Sorbet (Sorbet au Champagne)
Substitute Champagne, or any sparkling wine, for Sauternes.

Pear Sorbet

SORBET AUX POIRES

For a tarter sorbet to serve mid-meal instead of as dessert, double the amount of pear liqueur and halve the sugar.

MAKES 2 pt/1.25 litres – SERVES 6-8

5 oz/150 g caster sugar, more if needed	*4 tablespoons pear liqueur*
16 fl oz/475 ml water	*1 egg white*
juice of 2 lemons	**To serve**
1½ lb/750 g ripe pears	*pear liqueur*

ice-cream machine* or churn

In a saucepan heat sugar with water over a low heat until dissolved. Boil for 3 minutes, then stir in lemon juice. Peel and core the pears, cut into chunks and drop at once into lemon syrup to avoid discoloration. Cook the pears in syrup until transparent and very soft, 5-20 minutes depending on ripeness.

Drain pears and measure syrup, adding water as necessary to make 16 fl oz/475 ml. Purée pears in a food processor or blender and strain; the purée should also measure 16 fl oz/475 ml. Stir syrup back into purée with liqueur and taste, adding more sugar if needed. Chill mixture over ice and water or in the refrigerator until very cold. Taste it again.

Freeze the mixture in an ice-cream machine or churn, churning constantly until slushy. Whip egg white* until frothy, add to pear mixture and continue churning until firm. Pack into a chilled container, cover and freeze.

To serve: scoop sorbet into stemmed glasses and set glasses on plates. At table, pour a little pear liqueur over each serving.

GETTING AHEAD

Pear sorbet can be kept for up to 2 weeks, and should be frozen for at least 6 hours so that the flavour mellows. If frozen for more than 24 hours, move it to the refrigerator for an hour to soften before serving.

VARIATIONS

Blackcurrant Sorbet (Sorbet au cassis)
Substitute 1 lb/500 g blackcurrants for pears and cook thoroughly in sugar and water before puréeing; sieve the purée to remove seeds. Use blackcurrant liqueur instead of pear liqueur.

Calvados Sorbet (Sorbet au Calvados)
Substitute tart apples for pears and Calvados for pear liqueur.

Raspberry Sorbet

SORBET AUX FRAMBOISES

Frozen raspberries make good sorbets but less sugar is needed if the berries are already sweetened.

MAKES 1⅔ pt/1 litre – SERVES 4-6

5 oz/150 g caster sugar, more if needed

8 fl oz/250 ml water

1 lb/500 g fresh raspberries

2 tablespoons raspberry liqueur (framboise) or 1 tablespoon Kirsch or juice of ½ lemon, more if needed

1 egg white

To decorate

8 oz/250 g fresh raspberries

6-8 sprigs of mint

ice-cream machine* or churn

In a saucepan heat sugar with water over a low heat until dissolved. Boil sugar syrup* 3 minutes and let cool. Purée raspberries in a blender or food processor and strain to remove seeds; there should be ¾ pt/500 ml purée. Stir sugar syrup into purée with liqueur, Kirsch or lemon juice.

Chill the raspberry mixture over ice and water or in the refrigerator until very cold. Taste it, adding sugar or more liqueur if needed. Freeze the mixture in the ice-cream machine or churn, churning constantly until slushy.

Whip* egg white until frothy, add to sorbet and continue churning until firm. Cover and freeze.

To serve: shape the sorbet in ovals with 2 tablespoons, or use an ice-cream scoop. Set 3 ovals, points inwards, on chilled individual plates. Pile fresh raspberries in the centre, top with mint sprigs and serve at once.

GETTING AHEAD

Raspberry sorbet can be kept for up to 2 weeks, and should be frozen for at least 6 hours for the flavour to mellow. If frozen for more than 24 hours, move it to the refrigerator for an hour to soften before shaping and serving.

VARIATIONS

Peach Sorbet (Sorbet aux pêches)
Substitute 2 lb/1 kg ripe peaches for raspberries and flavour with Kirsch. Prepare syrup, adding juice of 2 lemons. Scald and peel peaches and slice directly into syrup to prevent discoloration, then purée with the syrup.

Melon Sorbet (Sorbet au melon)
Substitute a 3 lb/1.5 kg melon for raspberries and flavour with Kirsch or lemon juice. Reduce sugar and water by half.

Strawberry Sorbet (Sorbet aux fraises)
Substitute fresh strawberries for raspberries and flavour with Kirsch or lemon juice.

Lemon Sorbet in the Shell

CITRONS GIVREES

When frozen in the shell of the fruit, lemon sorbet absorbs flavour from the zest.

MAKES 12 FILLED LEMON HALVES
SERVES 6

7 lemons

5 oz/150 g caster sugar, more if needed

16 fl oz/475 ml water

egg white

To decorate

12 bay leaves

ice-cream machine* or churn

Cut 6 lemons in half crossways, then cut a generous slice from the base of each half so that they sit flat. Reserve the slice to use as a lid. Scoop out the flesh with a teaspoon and squeeze to extract the juice. Grate the rind and squeeze the juice of the remaining lemon. Measure 8 fl oz/250 ml juice, reserving the rest for another use. Freeze lemon shells.

In a saucepan heat sugar with water over low heat until dissolved. Boil sugar syrup 3 minutes and let cool. Stir into lemon juice and chill the mixture over ice and water or in the refrigerator until very cold. Taste, adding more sugar if needed.

Freeze the mixture in the ice-cream machine or churn, churning constantly until slushy. Whip* egg white until frothy, add to sorbet and continue churning until firm. Pack sorbet into lemon shells, mounding it well, and top with lids. Wrap and freeze.

To decorate: set 2 lemon halves on each of 6 small plates and top each with a bay leaf to imitate a lemon leaf.

GETTING AHEAD

Filled lemons can be kept for up to 2 weeks, and should be frozen for at least 6 hours so the flavour mellows. If frozen for more than 24 hours, move them to the refrigerator for 1 hour to soften before serving.

VARIATIONS

Lemon Mint Sorbet (Sorbet de citron à la menthe)
Add the crushed leaves of 1 bunch of mint (about 3 oz/90 g) to hot sugar syrup, cover and infuse over low heat, 10-15 minutes. Strain syrup before adding lemon juice. Serve sorbet in stemmed glasses.

Tangerine Sorbet in the Shell (Mandarines givrées)
Substitute tangerines for lemons, leaving shells whole with a single lid. Use 12 fl oz/350 ml juice with same proportions of other ingredients.

TEA AND LIME GRANITE

GRANITE AU THE ET AU CITRON VERT

Tea should be strongly brewed for granité.

MAKES 3¼ pt/2 litres – SERVES 6

6½ oz/200 g caster sugar, more if needed

2 pt/1.25 litres water

1 oz/30 g Ceylon or Indian tea

juice and grated zest of 3 limes

In a saucepan heat sugar with 8 fl oz/250 ml of the water over a low heat until dissolved. Boil sugar syrup* 3 minutes and let cool. Boil remaining water, pour over tea and leave 10 minutes. Strain and mix with sugar syrup, lime juice and zest.

Chill the mixture over ice and water or in the refrigerator until very cold. Taste, adding sugar if needed. Freeze the mixture until slushy. Whisk until smooth, then freeze again. Repeat until granité is firm; the texture will be quite grainy. Freeze for at least 1 hour.

To serve: pile granité into chilled stemmed glasses.

GETTING AHEAD

Granité can be frozen for up to 2 days but the texture will crystallize.

Before serving, break up crystals with the tines of a fork, or for a smoother texture work it briefly in a food processor.

VARIATIONS

Grape Juice Granité (Granité aux raisins)
Substitute 16 fl oz/475 ml fresh red or white grape juice for lime juice and tea, and use half the sugar or to taste. Serves 3.

Orange Granité (Granité à l'orange)
Substitute 16 fl oz/475 ml fresh orange juice for lime juice and tea, and use half the sugar or to taste. Serves 3.

—6—
CHOUX PASTRY

Choux pastry never fails to delight when it puffs like magic to golden crunchy balls three times their original size. It isn't magic at all of course, simply the action of heat on eggs which have been beaten into a flour, butter and water paste.

To make the dough, butter and water are brought just to the boil, then sifted flour is beaten in so the heat of the water cooks the flour to a paste. Within half a minute a smooth ball, technically called a panade, is formed, pulling away from the sides of the pan. The eggs are added one by one, again beaten in with plenty of vigour.

Adding the right amount of egg is vital. The more egg that is added, the better the dough will puff, but only up to a certain point. With too much egg, the dough is too soft to rise at all, so the last one is beaten in little by little to achieve a soft shiny dough which just drops from the spoon.

Choux is the odd man out among pastries for it is cooked twice, first when making the dough, and a second time when baked in the oven or, more rarely, deep-fried or poached in water. Cream puffs, éclairs, profiteroles and other classic recipes relying on choux pastry need little introduction. They all depend on fillings and icing (or a sauce) to give them character, and the classic flavours of vanilla, coffee and chocolate are hard to beat.

In summer choux goes well with raspberries or strawberries and a filling of Chantilly cream. In winter profiteroles with rum or pistachio ice-cream (p. 36) and hot chocolate sauce (p. 32) maintain a high profile. Whatever your preference, choux puffs fresh from the oven with the filling added just before they reach the table are a treat that is rarely found outside a home kitchen.

KEYS TO THE BEST CHOUX PASTRY

The butter and water mixture should be brought only just to the boil so that the water does not evaporate and change the proportions of the dough.

Add the flour all in one batch so that it cooks evenly.

Beat hard when adding the eggs. At the start, the eggs will thicken the dough slightly, then it will soften and take on a glossy sheen as the last one or two are added.

Choux pastry should be piped into smooth even shapes which rise well on the baking sheet. Never flatten the dough when piping, but let it fall naturally from the tube.

Space the pastries generously on the baking sheet so that each one has room to expand and dry well.

As they bake, first the pastries puff, then they must cook further until they become dry and crisp. They produce a good deal of steam; in an electric oven with no circulation of air, the door should be propped open slightly after 10 minutes cooking.

Do not open the oven wide during first 15 minutes baking. Half-cooked choux pastry collapses disastrously in a draught.

Choux puffs appear done before they are ready and golden colour is little indication. If you look at the cracks in the sides of the puffs, they should no longer be pale. Test by removing a puff and letting it cool; if it stays crisp, it is done.

Baked puffs are best eaten the day of baking but they can be stored for up to 2 days in an airtight container; if frozen, however, they tend to dry out. Once they are filled, choux pastries should be eaten within an hour or two as they soften rapidly.

CHOUX PASTRY

PATE A CHOUX

The most versatile of all pastry doughs.

MAKES 16-20 ECLAIRS

5 oz/150 g plain flour
8 fl oz/250 ml water
3/4 teaspoon salt
3 1/4 oz/100 g unsalted butter
4-5 eggs

Sift flour on to a piece of paper. In a saucepan heat water, salt and butter until butter is melted. Bring just to the boil and take from the heat. Add all flour at once and beat vigorously with a wooden spoon until the mixture is smooth and pulls away from the sides of the pan to form a ball, about 20 seconds. Beat for 1/2 minute over very low heat to dry the mixture. Take from heat and cool slightly.

Beat in eggs one at a time, beating well after each addition. Beat last egg with a fork in a small bowl and add it, little by little, to the dough. When enough egg has been added the dough will be shiny and just soft enough to fall from the spoon. *Note*: all the last egg may not be needed.

GETTING AHEAD

Choux pastry dough can be kept for up to 24 hours in the refrigerator. It can also be shaped and frozen ready for baking.

ECLAIRS

Eclairs can be filled with a choice of vanilla, chocolate or coffee pastry cream and topped with coffee or chocolate icing. I happen to think a combination of coffee and chocolate is the best.

MAKES 16-20

For choux pastry

5 oz/150 g plain flour

8 fl oz/250 ml water

¾ teaspoon salt

3 ¼ oz/100 g unsalted butter

4-5 eggs

1 egg, beaten with ½ teaspoon salt (for glaze)*

For coffee pastry cream

16 fl oz/475 ml milk

6 egg yolks

3 ¼ oz/100 g caster sugar

¾ oz/20 g plain flour

2 tablespoons dry instant coffee

For chocolate icing

1 ½ oz/45 g plain chocolate, chopped

4-5 tablespoons water

8 oz/250 g powdered sugar

few drops vanilla essence

pastry bag*
¾ in/2 cm and ¼ in/5 mm plain tubes*
pastry cases (optional)

Heat oven to gas 6/400°F/200°C. Lightly butter a baking sheet. Make choux pastry (p. 48).

Using the pastry bag and ¾ in/2 cm plain tube, pipe* 16-20 strips of choux pastry, about 4 in/10 cm long, on to baking sheet, leaving room for expansion. Brush dough with egg glaze and score top lengthways with a fork so that dough rises well.

Bake until crisp and brown, 25-30 minutes. Transfer to a rack and, while still warm, poke a hole at each end of base of éclairs, to allow steam to escape, using the small tube.

Make coffee pastry cream (p. 59). Using the pastry bag and ¼ in/5 mm plain tube, pipe* pastry cream into éclairs, filling them from each end.

For icing: melt chocolate on a heatproof plate over a pan of hot water. Whisk enough water into sugar to make a smooth paste that just coats the spoon; stir in melted chocolate and vanilla. *Note*: when tepid, the icing should just coat the back of a spoon; if too thick, add more water, or if too thin, beat in more sugar.

Prop bowl sideways and dip top of each éclair into icing, lifting it out with twist so it does not drip. Set éclairs on a plate for serving, in paper cases if you wish.

GETTING AHEAD

Eclairs can be baked up to 24 hours ahead and kept in an airtight container and pastry cream can be kept for up to 24 hours in the refrigerator. However, do not fill éclairs more than 4 hours ahead; if necessary dry them in a low oven so that they are crisp before filling.

VARIATIONS

Chantilly Eclairs (Eclairs Chantilly)
Fill éclairs with Chantilly cream*, made with 8 fl oz/250 ml double cream and flavoured with 1 tablespoon brandy or rum.

Praline Eclairs (Eclairs au pralin)
Fill éclairs with praline pastry cream (p. 59). Omit icing and sprinkle top with powdered sugar.

Chantilly Swans

CYGNES CHANTILLY

The swans can be served floating on a lake of raspberry sauce (p. 50) or on a silver tray or mirror to represent water.

MAKES 10

For choux pastry

5 oz/150 g plain flour

8 fl oz/250 ml water

3/4 teaspoon salt

3 1/4 oz/100 g unsalted butter

4-5 eggs

1 egg, beaten with 1/2 teaspoon salt (for glaze)*

15-20 almond sticks

To finish

Chantilly cream, made with 12 fl oz/350 ml double cream*

powdered sugar (for sprinkling)

pastry bag* and medium star tube*
1/2 in/1 cm and 1/4 in/5 mm plain tubes*

Heat oven to gas 6/400°F/200°C. Lightly butter 2 baking sheets. Make choux pastry (p. 48).

For swan bodies: using the pastry bag and 1/2 in/1 cm plain tube, pipe* 10 solid ovals of choux pastry, about 3 in/7 cm long, on to one baking sheet, leaving plenty of room for expansion. Brush ovals lightly with some of the egg glaze and bake until crisp and brown, 25-30 minutes. Transfer to a rack and, while still warm, slice bodies horizontally so that steam can escape. Cut tops in half lengthways to form wings.

Meanwhile, pipe* swan necks: press the 1/4 in/5 mm plain tube down to cover larger one and pipe* S shapes on to second baking sheet. Make extra necks to allow for breakage. Insert a stick of almond at one end of the S as beak.

Brush dough with egg glaze and bake until brown, 10-15 minutes. Transfer to a rack to cool. *Note*: bake necks in a separate oven, or wait until bodies are done.

To finish: using the pastry bag and star* tube, pipe* mounds of Chantilly cream to fill swan bodies. Set wings on each side, pointing upwards and outwards, with a neck upright in front. Sprinkle swans with powdered sugar and set on a tray. Keep in the refrigerator and serve within 2 hours.

GETTING AHEAD

Swans can be baked up to 24 hours ahead and kept in an airtight container. If pastry softens, dry it in a very low oven before filling.

VARIATIONS

Cream Puffs (Choux à la crème)
Pipe* dough in 2.5 in/6 cm mounds instead of ovals. Cut off lids when cooked and fill generously with Chantilly cream.

Strawberry Swans (Cygnes aux fraises)
Add a layer of sliced strawberries to swans with Chantilly cream.

Raspberry Sauce

SAUCE MELBA

Named for Dame Nellie Melba, of peach Melba as well as operatic fame.

MAKES 1/2 pt/300 ml

8 oz/250 g fresh or frozen raspberries

2 oz/60 g caster sugar (optional)

1 tablespoon Kirsch

Purée raspberries in a blender or food processor with sugar. *Note*: if frozen raspberries are already sweetened, more sugar may not be needed. Sieve to remove seeds. Chill sauce and stir in Kirsch just before serving.

GETTING AHEAD

Raspberry sauce can be kept for up to 3 days in the refrigerator, or can be frozen. Stir in Kirsch just before serving.

Profiteroles with Strawberry Coulis

PROFITEROLES AU COULIS DE FRAISES

A summer version of the familiar chocolate profiteroles.

SERVES 8

For choux pastry
5 oz/150 g plain flour
8 fl oz/250 ml water
¾ teaspoon salt
3¼ oz/100 g unsalted butter
4-5 eggs
1 egg, beaten with ½ teaspoon salt (for glaze)*
Chantilly cream, made with 8 fl oz/250 ml double cream*

To serve
strawberry coulis (p. 51)

---

pastry bag*
½ in/1 cm and ¼ in/5 mm plain tubes*

Heat oven to gas 6/400°F/200°C. Lightly butter 2 baking sheets. Make choux pastry (p. 48).

Using the pastry bag and ½ in/1 cm plain tube, pipe* 1 in/2.5 cm mounds of choux pastry well apart on baking sheets. Brush lightly with glaze and bake until crisp and brown, 20-25 minutes. Transfer profiteroles to a rack and, while still warm, poke a hole in base of profiteroles to allow steam to escape, using the small tube.

Not more than 2 hours before serving, fill profiteroles by piping Chantilly cream through hole in base with the pastry bag and ¼ in/5 mm plain tube. Pile filled profiteroles in a shallow bowl, or on individual plates.

To serve: spoon strawberry coulis over profiteroles to partly coat them and serve remaining coulis separately.

GETTING AHEAD

Profiteroles can be baked up to 24 hours ahead and stored in an airtight container.

VARIATIONS

Chocolate Profiteroles (Profiteroles au chocolat)
Split profiteroles and fill with vanilla ice-cream (p. 36) instead of Chantilly cream. Pour over hot chocolate sauce (p. 32) instead of strawberry coulis and serve at once.

Small Caramel Choux (Petits choux au caramel)
Fill profiteroles with Chantilly cream flavoured with 1 tablespoon brandy or Grand Marnier instead of vanilla. Make very light-coloured caramel* with 3¼ oz/100 g caster sugar and dip base of pan in hot water so that caramel remains liquid. Working quickly, dip tops of choux into caramel; it will set to a shiny glaze. Serve within 2 hours. If shaped as ovals, these choux are called salambôs.

Strawberry Ice-Cream Profiteroles
(Profiteroles à la glace aux fraises)
Split profiteroles and fill with strawberry ice-cream (p. 38) instead of Chantilly cream.

Strawberry Coulis

COULIS DE FRAISES

A happy end for any squashed berries.

MAKES ¾ pt/475 ml

1 lb/500 g strawberries, hulled and washed if sandy
3-4 tablespoons caster sugar, more if needed
1 tablespoon Kirsch or juice of ½ lemon

Purée strawberries in a food processor or blender with sugar and Kirsch or lemon juice. Strain coulis to remove seeds and taste, adding more sugar if needed, then chill.

GETTING AHEAD

Strawberry coulis can be kept for up to 3 days in the refrigerator, or can be frozen.

—7—
FRENCH PASTRY DOUGH

On Sundays in France, pastry shop windows blossom with a bevy of pies and tarts, fruit or plain, rich with cream or crunchy with nuts, golden brown and shiny with glaze. Yet a good home-made tart, arriving fresh from the oven, beats the best of these professional products any day.

Foundations of French tarts are pâte brisée – literally broken pastry – and its sweet version, pâte sucrée. Both doughs are mixed on a flat surface, then kneaded with the heel of the hand to "break" the dough and give it a characteristic putty-like texture.

Proportions of pâte brisée vary from recipe to recipe. An extra egg yolk will add richness, or a whole egg helps the dough keep its shape for deep pies. Less fat may be used if a tart filling is particularly moist or rich. Because of its flavour, butter is the fat most cooks prefer, but occasionally lard or shortening can take its place.

In pâte sucrée, the high proportion of sugar and egg yolks give the dough a luxuriously crumbly texture, so rich it can be baked alone as biscuits. Proportions of the dough vary less than for pâte brisée, but ground nuts can replace some of the flour, and grated lemon rind or liqueur may be added as flavouring instead of vanilla.

Variations in the dough are of minor importance compared with the filling and it is here that imagination counts. Apples, for instance, lend themselves to innumerable single- and double-crust pies, with the fruit sliced, chopped or puréed. Most berries look best in an open tart with plenty of glaze (redcurrant for red fruits, apricot for the rest), with perhaps a bed of pastry cream.

Fruits which discolour are poached before arranging in the pastry shell, then topped with a glaze made from the poaching syrup. Or the filling may be based on nuts, perhaps with no fruit at all. Every French cook has their own special recipes, and these are just a few ideas.

KEYS TO THE BEST PATE BRISEE AND PATE SUCREE

Unsalted butter is best for pastry as it contains less whey. If you are using salted butter in these recipes, reduce added salt by half.

After mixing, the dough should be left to rest in the refrigerator so that it loses elasticity and the butter sets, making it easier to roll.

Pâte brisée and pâte sucrée can be mixed in the food processor, but for the correct pliable consistency they must still be kneaded with the heel of the hand on a floured work surface.

When lining the tin with dough, shape high sides so that plenty of room is left for the filling. Chill the dough again so that it sets and keeps its shape in the oven.

To be sure that the bottom crust of a tart is thoroughly cooked, it helps to preheat a baking sheet and to set the tart down near the bottom of the oven.

Often a pastry shell is best baked empty (blind) so that it is not soaked by a moist filling.

Take care when baking pâte sucrée as it scorches easily because of the high proportion of sugar.

Baked pastry shells can be stored in an airtight container for a day or two. However, once a filling has been added, the sooner a tart is eaten the better, so that the pastry stays crisp.

PASTRY DOUGH

PATE BRISEE

The proportions of this recipe are often adjusted to use more or less butter or egg.

MAKES A 10 in/25 cm TART SHELL

6½ oz/200 g plain flour
3¼ oz/100 g unsalted butter
1 egg yolk
½ teaspoon salt
3 tablespoons water, more if needed

Sift flour on to a work surface and make a well in the centre.

With your fist pound the butter to soften it slightly. Add butter, egg yolk, salt and water to well and work with your fingertips until mixed.

Using a pastry scraper or metal spatula draw in flour and work until coarse crumbs are formed. If crumbs seem dry, add 1-2 tablespoons more water. Press dough into a ball; it should be soft but not sticky.

Lightly flour the work surface and blend the dough by pushing it away with the heel of your hand and gathering it up with a scraper. After 1-2 minutes, the dough should be as smooth as putty and peel easily from the work surface.

Press it into a ball, wrap and chill for 30 minutes.

GETTING AHEAD

Pâte brisée can be kept for up to 2 days in the refrigerator.

It can also be rolled, shaped and frozen for up to 2 months.

VARIATION

Savoury Pie Pastry (Pâte à pâté)
Substitute 1½ oz/45 g lard for half the butter. Use 1 whole egg instead of 1 egg yolk, and 1-2 tablespoons water.

Sweet Pastry Dough

PATE SUCREE

Good enough to bake on its own as biscuits.

MAKES A 10 in/25 cm TART SHELL

6½ oz/200 g plain flour, more if needed

3¼ oz/100 g unsalted butter

3¼ oz/100 g caster sugar

4 egg yolks

½ teaspoon salt

few drops vanilla essence

Sift flour on to a work surface and make a well in the centre. With your fist pound the butter to soften it slightly. Add butter, sugar, egg yolks, salt and vanilla essence to well and work with your fingertips until mixed.

Using a pastry scraper or metal spatula draw in flour and work until coarse crumbs are formed. Press the dough into a ball; if it is sticky, work in 2-3 tablespoons flour.

Lightly flour the work surface and blend dough by pushing it away with the heel of your hand and gathering it up with a scraper. After 1-2 minutes, the dough should be smooth and peel easily from the work surface. Press it into a ball, wrap and chill for 30 minutes.

GETTING AHEAD

Pâte sucrée can be kept for up to 2 days in the refrigerator.

It can also be rolled, shaped and frozen for up to 1 month.

VARIATIONS

Almond Pâte Sucrée (Pâte sucrée aux amandes)
Substitute 3 oz/90 g ground almonds for half the flour and omit 2 egg yolks. If you like, flavour dough with 1 tablespoon Kirsch.

Lemon Pâte Sucrée (Pâte frolle)
Substitute grated zest of 1 lemon for vanilla.

Plum Tart with Custard Topping

TARTE AUX PRUNES ALSACIENNE

The dough for this tart is made with whole egg, so it is drier and absorbs juice from the cooked fruit.

Breadcrumbs sprinkled in the bottom of this tart also help to keep the pastry crisp.

SERVES 6-8

For pâte brisée

6½ oz/200 g plain flour

3¼ oz/100 g unsalted butter

1 egg

½ teaspoon salt

1-2 tablespoons water, more if needed

For filling

1 oz/30 g dry breadcrumbs

1½ lb/750 g ripe plums, halved and stoned

1 egg

1 egg yolk

4 fl oz/125 ml double cream

2 oz/60 g caster sugar

powdered sugar (for sprinkling)

---

10 in/25 cm tart tin*

Make pâte brisée (p. 54) and chill. Put a baking sheet* in the oven and heat to gas 7/425°F/220°C. Roll out pastry dough and line* the tart tin. Sprinkle breadcrumbs in pastry shell and tightly pack plums on top, cut sides up. Set on the hot baking sheet and bake 10 minutes.

Meanwhile, whisk egg and egg yolk with cream and sugar until mixed. Pour mixture over fruit, reduce oven temperature to gas 4/350°F/180°C and continue baking until dough is browned, plums are tender and custard mixture is set, 30-35 minutes. *Note*: do not overbake or the custard will curdle.

Serve the tart warm or at room temperature

and, just before serving, sprinkle generously with powdered sugar.

GETTING AHEAD

Plum tart can be cooked a few hours ahead but is best eaten the day of baking.

VARIATIONS

Apricot Tart with Custard Topping
(Tarte aux abricots Alsacienne)
Substitute fresh apricots for plums, setting a halved almond in each apricot half.

Bilberry Tart with Custard Topping
(Tarte aux myrtilles Alsacienne)
Substitute bilberries for plums, picking them over and washing before adding to the pie shell. Sprinkle tart with 1 teaspoon ground cinnamon mixed with 2 tablespoons caster sugar just before serving.

Plum Tartlets with Custard Topping (Tartelettes aux prunes)
Roll pastry dough and line* 8-10 4 in/10 cm tartlet tins*. Add plums and bake tartlets, allowing 15-20 minutes cooking after adding custard.

Light Apple Tart

TARTE AUX POMMES LEGERE

Following the new-style cooking, this recipe uses a minimum of pastry and apples to make a wafer-thin, crisp tart.

SERVES 6

For pâte brisée
6½ oz/200 g plain flour
3¼ oz/100 g unsalted butter
½ teaspoon salt
1 egg yolk
3 tablespoons water, more if needed

For filling
6 dessert apples
1½ oz/45 g unsalted butter, melted
1½ oz/45 g caster sugar

Make pâte brisée (p. 54) and chill 30 minutes. Heat oven to gas 6/400°F/200°C.

Roll out dough as thinly as possible to a 15 in/40 cm square, cut it in half and set on 2 baking sheets*. Trim edges neatly. Peel, halve and core apples. Slice them as thinly as possible and arrange diagonally on the dough, starting in one corner and overlapping the slices slightly until dough is completely covered. The pastry burns easily if not completely covered with apples. Brush apples lightly with melted butter and sprinkle with half the sugar. Bake until pastry is crisp and apples are tender, 20-25 minutes. Sprinkle tart with remaining sugar and put under grill until sugar caramelizes, 2-3 minutes. Serve at once while still hot.

GETTING AHEAD

Light apple tart can be shaped up to an hour before baking. Keep it in the refrigerator, tightly covered.

VARIATION

Light Fig Tart (Tarte aux figues légère)
Substitute 12 fresh figs for apples, cutting them in ½ in/1 cm crossways slices.

Medieval Apple Pie

TOURTE AUX POMMES TAILLEVENT

This pie, filled with a kind of apple mincemeat, comes from a cookbook by Taillevent, chef to the kings of France in the late 14th century.

SERVES 10

For savoury pie pastry

13 oz/400 g plain flour

3¼ oz/100 g unsalted butter

3¼ oz/100 g lard or shortening

2 eggs

1 teaspoon salt

5-6 tablespoons water

For filling

2 onions, chopped

1½ oz/45 g unsalted butter

8 dessert apples

6 dried figs, chopped

5 oz/150 g dark raisins

8 fl oz/250 ml port or sweet white wine

2 teaspoons ground cinnamon

1 teaspoon ground ginger

1 teaspoon crushed aniseed

1 egg, beaten with ½ teaspoon salt (for glaze)*

10 in/25 cm spring-form tin*

Make savoury pie pastry (p. 54) and chill for 30 minutes. Fry onion in butter until very soft but not brown. Peel apples, core and coarsely grate them. At once mix with onion, figs, raisins, port or wine, cinnamon, ginger and aniseed.

Roll out two-thirds of pastry dough and line* the spring-form tin, overlapping edge of tin with dough. Spread filling in pastry and brush dough edges with some of glaze. Roll remaining dough to a 10 in/25 cm round and cover apple mixture. Roll rolling pin over edge of tin to cut off excess dough, then flute the edges to decorate and seal together.

Note: do not let dough overlap sides of tin.

Brush top of pie with egg glaze and cut 4 or 5 small holes with a knife to allow steam to escape. Roll out pastry trimmings and use to decorate pie with leaves, flowers, etc. Brush decorations with glaze and chill pie for 15-20 minutes. Put a baking sheet* in the oven and heat to gas 5/375°F/190°C. Set tart on hot baking sheet and bake until brown and the dough starts to shrink from sides of tin, 1-1¼ hours. Let pie cool to tepid before unmoulding and serve it warm or at room temperature.

GETTING AHEAD

Medieval apple pie can be baked 24 hours ahead and stored in an airtight container. Reheat in a low oven before serving.

VARIATION

Medieval Apple Pie with Fresh Fruits

(Tourte aux pommes et aux fruits frais Taillevent)

Substitute 8 oz/250 g halved and pipped red or green seedless grapes for raisins, and fresh figs for dried ones. Reduce port by half and sweeten the fruit mixture to taste with caster sugar.

FRESH FRUIT TART

TARTE AUX FRUITS FRAIS

Ideal for summer fruits like strawberries, raspberries and cherries; in winter a fresh fruit tart can be filled with grapes or oranges.

SERVES 8

For lemon pâte sucrée

6½ oz/200 g plain flour

3¼ oz/100 g unsalted butter

3¼ oz/100 g caster sugar

4 egg yolks

½ teaspoon salt

grated zest of 1 lemon

For liqueur pastry cream

16 fl oz/475 ml milk

1 vanilla pod or few drops vanilla essence

6 egg yolks

3½ oz/100 g caster sugar

¾ oz/20 g plain flour

knob of butter

2-3 tablespoons Kirsch or Grand Marnier

1 lb/500 g fresh fruit

8 fl oz/250 ml redcurrant jelly glaze or apricot jam glaze**

---

10 in/25 cm tart tin*

Make lemon pâte sucrée (p. 55) and chill for 30 minutes. Make liqueur pastry cream (p. 59). Heat oven to gas 6/400°F/200°C.

Hull strawberries; pick over raspberries; stone cherries; remove seeds from grapes but do not peel; peel oranges, removing all skin and pith, and slice them. Wash any fruit only if it is dirty as washing softens it.

Roll out pastry dough, line* the tart tin and bake blind*.

To finish: not more than 2 hours before serving, spread pastry cream in the tart shell. Arrange fruit in concentric circles on top. Melt glaze and brush on fruits and edge of pastry generously.

GETTING AHEAD

The tart shell can be stored for up to 2 days in an airtight container, and pastry cream can be kept for up to 2 days in the refrigerator. Prepare the fruit up to 8 hours ahead.

VARIATIONS

Almond Fruit Galette (Galette amandine aux fruits)
Make almond pâte sucrée (p. 55) and bake in a 12 in/30 cm round on a baking sheet*. Omit pastry cream and top pastry round with fruit and glaze*. Decorate with 1-2 tablespoons toasted* sliced almonds and pipe* rosettes of Chantilly cream* made with 4 fl oz/125 ml double cream.

Fruit Tartlets (Tartelettes aux fruits)
Shape 8-10 3 in/7 cm tartlet shells and bake blind*. Omit pastry cream, fill shells with fruit and glaze them.

Simple Fruit Tart (Tarte aux fruits simple)
Omit pastry cream and fill shell only with fruit and glaze.

VANILLA PASTRY CREAM

CREME PATISSIERE A LA VANILLE

Many pastry chefs prefer to lighten this basic pastry cream by adding Italian meringue (p. 82) which is a bit sweet for my taste, or whipped Chantilly cream*.

MAKES 1 pt/600 ml

16 fl oz/475 ml milk

1 vanilla pod or few drops vanilla essence

6 egg yolks

3¼ oz/100 g caster sugar

¾ oz/20 g plain flour

knob of butter

Bring milk just to the boil. If using vanilla pod add it, cover the pan and leave over low heat to infuse, 10-15 minutes.

Meanwhile, whip egg yolks with sugar* until thick and light, about 2 minutes. Stir in flour. Strain milk into egg yolks, reserving vanilla pod to use again, and stir to mix.

Return mixture to pan and bring to the boil, whisking constantly. *Note*: be sure cream is smooth before letting it boil and thicken. If lumps form as it thickens, take at once from the heat and whisk until smooth.

Cook cream gently, whisking constantly, until it thins slightly, showing the flour is completely cooked, about 2 minutes. *Note*: if cream is undercooked it tastes of flour. Take from heat and, if using vanilla essence, add it now.

Transfer cream to a bowl and rub knob of butter on top to prevent a skin forming. Cover and let cool.

GETTING AHEAD

Pastry cream can be kept for up to 2 days in the refrigerator, tightly covered. Thick pastry cream can be frozen, but if it is thin it will separate.

VARIATIONS

Chocolate Pastry Cream
(Crème pâtissière au chocolat)
On a heatproof plate over a pan of hot water, melt 6 oz/175 g plain chocolate, chopped, and beat into vanilla pastry cream.

Coffee Pastry Cream (Crème pâtissière au café)
Dissolve 2 tablespoons dry instant coffee in the milk.

Light Pastry Cream (Crème pâtissière légère)
Add to any flavour of pastry cream, Chantilly cream* made with 8 fl oz/250 ml double cream. Fold* together as lightly as possible.

Liqueur Pastry Cream (Crème pâtissière au liqueur)
Add 2-3 tablespoons Grand Marnier, Kirsch, rum, etc. to taste.

Pastry Cream with Meringue (Crème chibouste)
Fold* Italian meringue (p. 82), made with 2 egg whites, into any flavour of pastry cream.

Praline Pastry Cream (Crème pâtissière au pralin)
Add praline* made with 3 oz/90 g whole unblanched almonds.

LEMON TART

TARTE AU CITRON

A Provençale speciality.

SERVES 6

For pâte sucrée

6½ oz/200 g plain flour

3¼ oz/100 g unsalted butter

3¼ oz/100 g caster sugar

4 egg yolks

½ teaspoon salt

few drops vanilla essence

For filling

2 eggs

3¼ oz/100 g caster sugar

grated zest and juice of 1½ lemons

4 oz/125 g unsalted butter, melted

2 oz/60 g ground almonds

To decorate

candied slices from 2 lemons*

10 in/25 cm tart tin*

Make pâte sucrée (p. 55) and chill for 30 minutes. Heat oven to gas 5/375°F/190°C. Roll out pastry dough, line* the tart tin and bake blind* until firm but not brown.

For filling: whip eggs and sugar* until light and thick enough to leave a ribbon trail* when whisk is lifted, 4-5 minutes. Stir in lemon zest and juice, followed by melted butter and ground almonds.

Pour filling into tart shell and bake until filling is golden brown and set, 25-30 minutes.

Transfer tart to a rack to cool, then decorate with candied lemon slices.

GETTING AHEAD

Lemon tart is best eaten the day it is baked, but it can be kept for up to 24 hours in an airtight container.

Almond Tartlets

TARTELETTES AUX AMANDES

The filling for these tartlets puffs in the oven, but subsides again as it cools.

MAKES 12-14

For pâte sucrée

6½ oz/200 g plain flour

3¼ oz/100 g unsalted butter

3¼ oz/100 g caster sugar

4 egg yolks

½ teaspoon salt

few drops vanilla essence

For filling

2 eggs

3¼ oz/100 g caster sugar

2 oz/60 g ground almonds

1 tablespoon double cream

To decorate

about 40 blanched almond halves*

*4 fl oz/125 ml apricot glaze**

12-14 3 in/7 cm tartlet tins*

Make pâte sucrée (p. 55) and chill for 30 minutes. Butter the tartlet tins. Roll out dough thinly, line* tins and chill for 15 minutes. Put a baking sheet* in oven and heat to gas 5/375°F/190°C.

For filling: whip eggs with sugar* until light and thick, 4-5 minutes. Stir in ground almonds and cream. Spoon mixture into tartlet shells, to three-quarters full.

Set tins on heated baking sheet and bake tartlets for 15 minutes. Take from oven and add 3 almond halves, pointing inwards, on centre of each tartlet. Continue baking until lightly browned and filling is set, 10-15 minutes more. Transfer tins to a rack to cool.

Melt apricot glaze and brush over tartlets to glaze. Serve warm or at room temperature.

GETTING AHEAD

Almond tartlets are best eaten the day they are baked, but they can be kept for up to 3 days in an airtight container.

VARIATIONS

Hazelnut Tartlets (Tartelettes aux noisettes)
Substitute toasted* and peeled ground hazelnuts for almonds. Put 1 teaspoon honey in each tartlet shell before adding filling.

Maids of Honour (Demoiselles d'honneur)
Add 1 teaspoon raspberry jam to each tartlet shell before adding filling.

Pear Almond Tartlets
(Tartelettes aux poires amandine)
Halve the quantity of almond filling. Peel, quarter and core 3-4 ripe pears. Thinly slice them crossways. Spoon filling into tartlet shells, set pear slices on top and press down so that they are half covered. Bake and glaze.

Poached Fruit Tart

TARTE AUX FRUITS POCHES

This recipe suits peaches, pears, figs, apricots and other fruits which discolour when peeled. For the glaze, choose redcurrant jelly or apricot jam, depending on the colour of the fruit.

SERVES 8

For pâte sucrée

6 ½ oz/200 g plain flour

3 ¼ oz/100 g unsalted butter

3 ¼ oz/100 g caster sugar

4 egg yolks

½ teaspoon salt

few drops vanilla essence

For liqueur pastry cream

16 fl oz/475 ml milk

1 vanilla pod or few drops vanilla essence

6 egg yolks

3 ¼ oz/100 g caster sugar

¾ oz/20 g plain flour

2-3 tablespoons Kirsch or Grand Marnier

1 ½ lb/750 g fruit, poached and syrup reserved*

For glaze*

4 tablespoons redcurrant jelly or apricot jam

1 tablespoon arrowroot or cornflour, mixed to a paste with 3 tablespoons water

---

10 in/25 cm tart tin*

Make pâte sucrée (p. 55) and chill for 30 minutes. Make liqueur pastry cream (p. 59).

For glaze: boil syrup from poached fruit until reduced to 4 fl oz/125 ml. Stir in redcurrant jelly or apricot jam until melted. Strain glaze, return to the pan and bring to the boil. Whisk in arrowroot paste until glaze thickens, then take from heat.

Heat oven to gas 6/400°F/200°C. Roll out pastry dough, line* the tart tin and bake blind*.

To finish: not more than 2 hours before serving, spread pastry cream in tart shell. Arrange fruit in concentric circles on top. Melt glaze and brush fruits and edge of pastry generously.

GETTING AHEAD

Tart shell can be stored for up to 2 days in an airtight container, and pastry cream can be kept for up to 2 days in the refrigerator. Poached fruit and glaze can be prepared a day ahead and refrigerated.

VARIATIONS

Almond Poached Fruit Tart
(Tarte aux fruits pochés amandine)
Make tart shell with almond pâte sucrée (p. 55) and omit pastry cream. Decorate tart with blanched* almond halves.

Poached Fruit Tartlets (Tartelettes aux fruits)
Shape 8-10 3 in/7 cm tartlets and bake blind*. Fill with pastry cream, top with fruit and glaze.

8
PUFF PASTRY

The essence of culinary elegance, puff pastry poses a series of challenges which are neatly, triumphantly overcome by the cook. Ideally puff pastry should rise in the oven to four or five times its original thickness, to a flaky tower of nearly 1000 layers of dough interleaved with butter. This is done with the help of the most powerful raising agent of all – steam.

Operations start by mixing flour with water to a dough (called a *détrempe*) and wrapping it around a cake of butter, thus keeping the two as separate as possible. The package is rolled in a long strip, folded and rolled again, half a dozen times in all, until the layers compound to the magic four-figure multiple.

Every technique involved in making puff pastry – thorough chilling, resting between rollings to reduce elasticity, keeping corners square – is designed to keep the layers even and separate. When rolling and cutting into shape, again the most important consideration is to produce even layers that are free to rise.

In the oven, high heat converts the water in the *détrempe* to steam, separating the buttery layers and puffing them apart. Further cooking dries and toasts the dough to a golden crust that can be stacked in layers, as in mille-feuilles; may enclose a filling for turnovers or a *dartois*; or can form its own hollow case as a feuilleté. So delicious is the pastry itself that the finishes and fillings it requires are minimal – whipped cream, fruit, or simply caramelized sugar, toasted with the pastry as it bakes.

Puff pastry may not always be perfect, but I've never known it to fail to rise at all and I long ago ceased to be intimidated by it. So many perennials of the French repertoire depend on it that it's well worth a try or two to reach success.

KEYS TO THE BEST PUFF PASTRY

Adding lemon juice and a walnut-sized piece of butter to the *détrempe* cuts gluten and discourages the flour from becoming elastic.

The butter is pounded until pliable before wrapping in the *détrempe*; the closer the two are in consistency, the easier the dough is to roll.

The dough must be kept very cold. It helps to chill the work surface with a roasting tin of ice.

Work the dough as fast as possible and don't be afraid to treat it roughly.

If the dough starts to stick, stop rolling, dust it generously with flour and chill until firm, for up to an hour if necessary.

When shaping finished dough, trim 1 in/2.5 cm from the edges to remove folds. These trimmings are fine to make pastries like palm leaves (p. 65), which need not rise evenly.

To avoid sticking layers together, use a sharp knife when cutting and shaping dough. Do not let glaze or water drip down the sides.

Bake puff pastry on a dampened baking sheet. Water glues dough to the baking sheet so it shrinks less, and steam helps it to rise.

Chill dough thoroughly before baking so it retains its shape in the oven. Chilling sets the butter and gives the dough time to lose elasticity, so it shrinks less.

Puff pastry is baked in a very hot oven so dough puffs before butter can melt. Then the heat is lowered later, if necessary, to finish cooking.

Puff pastry should be very thoroughly browned. Toasting adds flavour as well as crispness.

Baked puff pastry can be kept for 2-3 days in an airtight container. After storage it is often improved by warming in the oven to crisp it.

PUFF PASTRY

PATE FEUILLETEE

Use the best unsalted butter for puff pastry, as it has the lowest water content.

MAKES 8-10 FEUILLETES

12 oz/375 g plain flour
12 oz/375 g unsalted butter, chilled
1 ½ teaspoons salt
1 ½ teaspoons lemon juice
6 fl oz/175 ml water, more if needed

To make *détrempe*: sift flour on to a chilled marble slab or work surface, and make a well in the centre. Add a walnut-sized piece of butter, salt, lemon juice and water and mix quickly with your fingertips. Using a pastry scraper or metal spatula, gradually draw in flour, working with the fingertips of both hands to form coarse crumbs. Add more water if the crumbs seem dry, then cut and turn with the scraper to form a rough, slightly moist ball of dough. Wrap and chill for 15 minutes.

Lightly flour the remaining butter and pound with a rolling pin, flattening and folding it until pliable. Shape into a 6 in/15 cm square.

Roll out *détrempe* to a 12 in/30 cm square, slightly thicker in the centre than at the sides. Place butter in the centre and wrap dough like a parcel, pinching the edges together. Set the parcel, seam side down, on a floured board and tap several times with the rolling pin to flatten it.

Roll out dough to a rectangle about 7 in/18 cm wide and 20 in/50 cm long, keeping corners square. Fold the rectangle in 3, like a business letter, to form a square of dough. Gently press the seams with a rolling pin to seal them and turn the dough a quarter turn to bring the seam side to your left. This is called a turn. Repeat the rolling and folding process once to give a second turn. Wrap and chill for 15 minutes. Give the dough 2 more turns, wrap and chill again. Finally give the dough 2 further turns to make a total of 6 and chill for a least 1 hour before using.

GETTING AHEAD

Puff pastry can be prepared through 4 turns and kept for up to 24 hours in the refrigerator or can be frozen. Give it 2 turns just before shaping.

VARIATION

Quick Puff Pastry (Pâte feuilletée simple)

When making *détrempe*, add one-third of butter instead of a walnut-sized piece. Roll out this dough to a rectangle and dot remaining butter over two-thirds of surface. Fold dough in thirds to enclose butter, seal, give dough one turn and chill for 15 minutes. Give dough two more turns and chill for 15 minutes before using.

PALM LEAVES

PALMIERS

When shaped very small, *palmiers* can be served as petits fours.

MAKES ABOUT 40

For puff pastry

12 oz/375 g plain flour

12 oz/375 g butter

1 ½ teaspoons salt

1 ½ teaspoons lemon juice

6 fl oz/175 ml water, more if needed

3 ¼ oz/100 g caster sugar (for rolling and sprinkling).

Make puff pastry (p. 64), giving it 4 turns, and chill for 15 minutes. Give dough 2 more turns, sprinkling work surface and dough with sugar instead of flour. Chill for 1 hour. Sprinkle 2 baking sheets* with water.

Roll out dough, again using sugar, to a rectangle, 10 × 18 in/25 × 45 cm and trim the edges. Fold one long edge over twice to reach centre of dough. Repeat on the other side and press lightly to seal with a rolling pin. Fold one rolled section of dough on top of the other and press again.

With a sharp knife cut dough into ⅜ in/1 cm slices. Lay slices on baking sheets, leaving room for them to puff. Curl top of slices slightly outwards to encourage them to expand. Chill for 15 minutes. Heat oven to gas 7/425°F/220°C.

Bake palm leaves until puffed and undersides are brown and caramelized, 8-10 minutes. Turn and brown other sides, 8-10 minutes more. *Note*: the pastries should be thoroughly browned and crisp, but be careful because the sugar burns easily. Transfer *palmiers* to a rack to cool.

GETTING AHEAD

Palmiers can be stored for up to a week in an airtight container. If they soften, dry them out in a low oven before serving.

VARIATIONS

Butterflies (Papillons)

Cut dough rectangle into 3 lengthways strips and pile one on top of another. With handle of a knife make a deep lengthways crease down the centre. With a sharp knife, cut into forty ⅜ in/1 cm slices. Twist each one once, set on baking sheet and chill before baking.

Matchsticks (Allumettes)

Make royal icing by whipping 1 egg white* until stiff, then beating in 6 oz/180 g powdered sugar or enough to make a stiff paste. Flavour with juice of ½ lemon. Spread dough rectangle with icing and cut into 2 lengthways strips. Cut strips crossways into 1 in/2.5 cm strips, set on baking sheet and chill before baking. Makes 24 matchsticks.

Almond Straws (Sacristains)

Brush dough rectangle with egg glaze* and sprinkle with 5 oz/150 g chopped almonds and 2 oz/60 g caster sugar. Cut dough into 2 lengthways strips, then cut these strips crossways into ¾ in/2 cm slices. Twist slices several times and set on baking sheet, pressing ends down well so twists do not unroll. Chill before baking.

MILLE-FEUILLES

MILLE-FEUILLES

A light version of the classic favourite.

SERVES 6-8

For puff pastry

8 oz/250 g plain flour

8 oz/250 g unsalted butter

1 teaspoon salt

1 teaspoon lemon juice

4 fl oz/125 ml water, more if needed

For vanilla pastry cream

16 fl oz/475 ml milk

1 vanilla pod or few drops vanilla essence

6 egg yolks

3¼ oz/100 g caster sugar

¾ oz/20 g plain flour

powdered sugar (for sprinkling)

metal skewer

Make puff pastry (p. 64) and chill for 1 hour. Dampen a baking sheet*. Roll out dough as thinly as possible to a rectangle, 15 in/40 cm wide and 18 in/45 cm long. Lay dough on baking sheet, prick all over with a fork and chill for 15 minutes. Heat oven to gas 7/425°F/220°C.

Bake dough until brown, 10-15 minutes. Turn dough over with a spatula and continue baking until very brown, 7-10 minutes more. *Note*: to add flavour the pastry should be thoroughly browned. While still warm, trim edges of pastry and cut it lengthways into 3 strips. Transfer to a rack to cool. Crush trimmings to crumbs.

Make vanilla pastry cream (p. 58). Spread half the pastry cream on one strip of pastry and top with another. Spread remaining cream on top and add the last pastry strip, pressing it down lightly. With a metal spatula smooth pastry cream around all sides and press on pastry crumbs to coat the pastry cream.

Sprinkle top thickly with powdered sugar. Heat the metal skewer on a burner until red hot and mark the sugar, making a lattice pattern of caramel. Cut mille-feuille crossways into slices and serve chilled or at room temperature.

GETTING AHEAD

The pastry strips can be baked up to 48 hours ahead and kept in an airtight container, while the mille-feuille itself can be assembled up to 2 hours before serving.

VARIATIONS

Chestnut Mille-Feuilles (Mille-feuilles aux marrons)
Flavour pastry cream with 2-3 tablespoons rum. Sandwich pastry layers with rum pastry cream and sprinkle with 1 lb/500 g coarsely crumbled commercial candied chestnuts (marrons glacés). For topping, melt 3 oz/90 g plain chocolate, chopped, on a heatproof plate over a pan of hot water, stir in ½ teaspoon oil and spread on the final pastry layer before putting it on top of the mille-feuille.

Classic Mille-Feuilles (Mille-feuilles classiques)
Sandwich the bottom 2 pastry layers with 6 oz/180 g raspberry jam, then add a layer of Chantilly cream* made with 12 fl oz/350 ml double cream. Coat the final layer of pastry with glacé icing* before putting it on top of the mille-feuille.

Fruit Mille-Feuilles (Mille-feuilles aux fruits)
Flavour pastry cream with 2-3 tablespoons Kirsch. Add 1 lb/500 g sliced strawberries or raspberries to the layers of pastry cream.

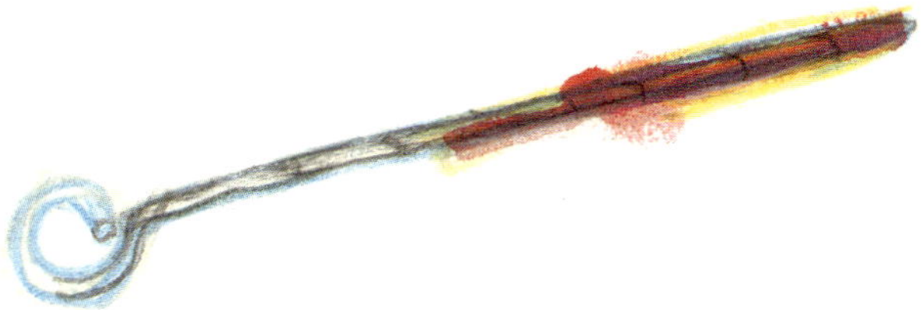

Puff Pastry Band with Almond Filling

DARTOIS AUX AMANDES

Be sure to seal the layers of dough carefully so that the filling cannot escape.

SERVES 8

For puff pastry

8 oz/250 g plain flour

8 oz/250 g unsalted butter

1 teaspoon salt

1 teaspoon lemon juice

4 fl oz/125 ml water, more if needed

For almond filling

4 oz/125 g unsalted butter

4½ oz/135 g caster sugar

1 egg

1 egg yolk

4 oz/125 g ground almonds

½ oz/15 g plain flour

1 tablespoon rum (optional)

1 egg, beaten with ½ teaspoon salt (for glaze)*

Make puff pastry (p. 64) and chill for 1 hour. For filling: cream butter, add sugar and beat until soft and light. Beat in egg and egg yolk. Stir in ground almonds, flour and rum, if using. *Note*: do not beat or almonds will become oily.

Dampen a baking sheet*. Roll out dough to a rectangle, 18 in/45 cm long and 10 in/25 cm wide. Trim edges and cut rectangle in half lengthways. Transfer one half to baking sheet and spoon almond mixture down the centre, leaving a 1 in/2.5 cm border. Brush border with some of egg glaze and set second dough rectangle on top. Press layers of dough firmly together and scallop edges with a knife.

Brush top with remaining egg glaze and lightly score with knife. Cut 5 or 6 small holes for steam to escape through top layer of dough. Chill for 15 minutes. Heat oven to gas 8/450°F/230°C.

Bake band until puffed and beginning to brown, 10-15 minutes. Reduce oven temperature to gas 5/375°F/190°C and continue baking until pastry is thoroughly browned, 20-25 minutes more. Transfer to a rack to cool. Cut band crossways into slices and serve warm or at room temperature.

GETTING AHEAD

Puff pastry band can be kept for 24 hours in an airtight container, or can be frozen. Warm in a low oven before serving. The band can also be shaped and frozen, then baked to serve.

VARIATIONS

Puff Pastry Band with Jam (Jalousie à la confiture)
Substitute 6-8 tablespoons raspberry, strawberry or other red jam for almond filling. Fold second dough rectangle in half lengthways and make a series of ⅜ in/1 cm cuts along the fold, leaving a 1 in/2.5 cm border. Transfer to first layer of dough and unfold it on top of jam. When baked, jam will show through slits in dough to resemble the louvres of a shutter, a *jalousie* in French.

Puff Pastry Band with Rum Cream
(Dartois au rhum)
Substitute almond filling with vanilla pastry cream (p. 58) flavoured with 2-3 tablespoons rum.

Note: Quick puff pastry may be substituted for puff pastry.

Cherry Turnovers

CHAUSSONS AUX CERISES

When cherries are out of season, black cherry jam can be substituted for fresh cherry filling.

MAKES 16

For puff pastry

12 oz/375 g plain flour

12 oz/375 g unsalted butter

1 ½ teaspoons salt

1 ½ teaspoons lemon juice

6 fl oz/175 ml water, more if needed

For filling

1 lb/500 g dark cherries, stoned

1 oz/30 g caster sugar

juice of ½ lemon

1 egg, beaten with ½ teaspoon salt (for glaze)*

4 in/10 cm fluted pastry cutter (optional)

Make puff pastry (p. 64) and chill for 1 hour. Sprinkle a baking sheet* with water.

For filling: put cherries in a heavy saucepan with sugar and lemon juice. Heat gently until juice runs, then simmer until cherries are tender and syrup is thick, 15-20 minutes. Let cool.

Roll out pastry dough until ⅛ in/3 mm thick. Stamp out rounds with the fluted cutter, or cut around a small pan lid. Brush edges with some of egg glaze and put a spoonful of cold cherry mixture in one centre of each round. *Note*: do not overfill or turnovers will burst. Fold over rounds to make semicircles, press edges firmly to seal, then flute them.

Transfer turnovers to baking sheet and brush with egg glaze. With point of a knife pierce 2-3 holes in the top of each to allow steam to escape. Chill for 15 minutes. Heat oven to gas 7/425°F/220°C. Bake turnovers until browned and crisp, about 20-25 minutes. Serve warm or at room temperature.

GETTING AHEAD

Turnovers can be stored for up to 24 hours in an airtight container. Warm them in a low oven before serving.

VARIATIONS

Apple Turnovers (Chaussons aux pommes)
Substitute apple filling for cherries: peel, core and slice 1 lb/500 g apples. Melt ½ oz/15 g butter in a frying pan, add apples and sprinkle with ½ oz/15 g caster sugar. Toss to coat with sugar, then fry briskly until apples brown and caramelize, tossing often. Add 1-2 tablespoons Calvados or brandy and flame. Let filling cool before using.

Peach Turnovers (Chaussons aux pêches)
Substitute peaches in apple filling above and flame with Kirsch.

Pear Turnovers (Chaussons aux poires)
Substitute pears in apple filling above and flame with pear brandy or Kirsch.

Note: Quick puff pastry may be substituted for puff pastry.

FEUILLETES WITH STRAWBERRIES

FEUILLETES AUX FRAISES

A diamond-shaped pastry case is much quicker to make than the traditional round *bouchée*.

MAKES 10 FEUILLETES

For puff pastry

12 oz/375 g plain flour

12 oz/375 g unsalted butter

1 ½ teaspoons salt

1 ½ teaspoons lemon juice

6 fl oz/175 ml water, more if needed

For filling

1 ½ lb/750 g strawberries

1-2 tablespoons caster sugar

1 egg, beaten with ½ teaspoon salt (for glaze)*

To finish

Chantilly cream, made with 8 fl oz/250 ml double cream*

1-2 tablespoons Kirsch

pastry bag* and medium star tube*

Make puff pastry (p. 64) and chill for 1 hour. Sprinkle a baking sheet* with water. Wash strawberries only if sandy. Hull them, reserving 10 for decoration. Slice hulled strawberries, sprinkle with caster sugar and leave to macerate.

Roll dough to a rectangle, 10 × 18 in/25 × 45 cm, and trim the edges. Cut dough in 3 lengthways strips and cut 3 diamonds from each strip. Shape leftovers into a tenth diamond. Set them on prepared baking sheet and brush with egg glaze.

With a sharp knife trace a line about ⅜ in/1 cm inside the edge of each diamond, cutting about half-way through the dough. In the same way, but not quite so deeply, mark a strawberry shape on each pastry. Chill for 15 minutes. Heat oven to gas 8/450°F/230°C. Bake feuilletés for 8 minutes. Reduce oven temperature to gas 5/375°F/190°C and continue baking until brown and crisp, 12-15 minutes. Transfer feuilletés to a rack, lift out centre of each pastry to form a lid and scoop out any soft dough with a teaspoon. Leave pastry to cool. To finish: not more than 2 hours before serving, flavour Chantilly cream with Kirsch. Half fill feuilletés with cream and add sliced strawberries. Using the pastry bag, pipe* rosettes of remaining Chantilly cream to cover strawberries. Set a whole strawberry to one side of each case and tip a lid sideways on top.

GETTING AHEAD

Feuilletés can be stored for up to 48 hours in an airtight container, or can be shaped, and frozen before being baked. Make Chantilly cream and fill feuilletés not more than 2 hours before serving.

VARIATIONS

Feuilletés with Peaches and Raspberry Sauce (Feuilletés Melba)
Omit strawberries and Chantilly cream. Halve and poach* 1 lb/500 g peaches. Drain, peel, stone and slice them. Warm feuilletés in oven. Spread vanilla ice-cream (p. 36) into base of feuilletés and top with overlapping slices of peach. Coat with a little raspberry sauce (p. 50), set a pastry lid at side of each and serve at once, with remaining sauce.

Feuilletés with Pears and Chocolate Sauce (Feuilletés Belle Hélène)
Omit strawberries and Chantilly cream. Peel, halve and core 1 lb/500 g pears. Poach* them and cut in slices. Warm feuilletés in oven. Spread vanilla ice-cream (p. 36) into base of feuilletés and top with overlapping slices of pear. Coat with a little hot chocolate sauce (p. 32), set a pastry lid at side of each and serve at once.

Feuilletés with Figs (Feuilletés aux figues)
Omit strawberries. Cut puff pastry dough into 10 rounds with a 4 in/10 cm round cutter instead of cutting in diamonds. Half fill feuilletés with Chantilly cream, slice 10 fresh figs and arrange overlapping on top of cream. Decorate figs with rosettes of cream and set a pastry lid at side of each, at an angle.

—9—
GENOISE AND CAKES

The French love to dress up their cakes. Plain pound cakes and sponges do exist, but, given the chance, a filling or an icing, and of course a fanciful decoration, are added to create a work of art from quite a simple batter.

Rarely is baking powder used in France, so that cakes rely on beaten eggs for lightness. Most popular is genoise, in which whole eggs are whisked with sugar to make a classic mousse thick enough to leave a ribbon trail, then folded with flour and a small amount of softened butter. The "biscuit" method is similar, but the eggs are separated, with the yolks beaten with sugar to a thick mousse and the whites made into meringue. A biscuit cake is lighter, but slightly drier than genoise. Ground almonds or walnuts can be added to either batter, but the basic methods of mixing remain the same.

The permutations of these basic cakes with half a dozen fillings and frostings almost need a computer to sort them out, but in practice the field narrows to popular combinations like genoise filled with coffee butter cream topped with toasted almonds, or chocolate roll with a mint or orange filling.

New ideas with a light touch include cakes filled with pastry cream or a mousse mixture of orange, pineapple and strawberry, instead of the heavier butter cream versions. Butter cream itself, or pastry cream, is often lightened with Italian meringue or Chantilly cream (the problem with the latter being that it does not hold for more than a couple of hours).

It is with decoration that the fun starts. Most fillings lend themselves to flat, smooth coatings as well as to shaped rosettes and ruffs. Toasted nuts, chocolate shapes, fresh and candied fruits are just a few possible extras. Lest these should get out of hand, bear in mind that a decoration should convey clues to the basic ingredients in a cake, and should always be edible. Please no ribbons or snowmen!

KEYS TO THE BEST GENOISE AND CAKES

Choose a cake tin of the correct shape and size, for batter bakes quite differently in too large or too small a tin.

Oven temperature is equally important; a small deviation can make a big difference in baking.

FREEZOMINT

Prepare ahead, heating the oven, lining cake tins and weighing ingredients before starting to mix a batter.

The trickiest part of making genoise and biscuit cake batter is adding the butter and this is always done last of all.

Small amounts can be melted but large amounts should be softened in a bowl over hot water to a pourable cream about the same consistency as the basic batter.

So that a cake cooks evenly, the shelf should be set about a third from the bottom of the oven. If baking 2 cakes, put them side by side rather than on 2 different shelves.

If a cake starts to brown too quickly, turn down the heat and cover it with a sheet of foil.

After baking, most cakes should be turned out at once so moisture can escape as they cool. Exceptions are delicate cakes, which might collapse, and rolled cakes, which are deliberately covered to keep them moist.

Plain sponge cakes become dry on keeping, but if they contain butter or nuts they keep well in an airtight container.

All of them freeze well.

How long you can store finished gâteaux depends very much on the filling.

Butter cream cakes can be kept for 3 days or more (one reason for their popularity) and their flavour will mellow.

Pastry cream, with or without Italian meringue to lighten it, lasts well for a couple of days, as do mousse mixtures.

However, any filling with Chantilly cream must be served within 2-3 hours.

If you are planning to keep a cake, finishing touches are best added at the last minute. However carefully you store them, piped rosettes and coatings of nuts tend to get tired after a day or two.

GENOISE

GENOISE

Alternatives to vanilla flavouring are the grated zest of 1 lemon or 1 orange, 1 teaspoon of orange flower water, or 2-3 drops anise oil.

MAKES ONE 9 in/23 cm CAKE

3 oz/90 g plain flour
pinch of salt
1 ½ oz/45 g unsalted butter
3 eggs
3 oz/90 g caster sugar
few drops vanilla essence

9 in/23 cm sloping-sided cake tin*

Butter the cake tin, line base with a round of greaseproof paper and butter the paper. Sprinkle tin with flour, discarding the excess.

Sift flour with salt. Warm butter in a bowl over a pan of hot water until it is soft enough to pour. *Note*: do not melt it into oil. Heat oven to gas 4/350°F/180°C.

Whip eggs and sugar* until light and thick enough to leave a ribbon trail* when whisk is lifted, then stir in vanilla essence. Sift flour over egg mixture and fold* in as lightly as possible. When almost mixed, add butter and gently fold into batter. *Note*: once butter is added, the batter loses volume quickly.

Pour batter into prepared tin and bake until cake is done*, 25-30 minutes. Run a knife around sides of cake and turn it out on to a rack to cool, peeling off paper.

GETTING AHEAD

Genoise can be kept for up to 2-3 days in an airtight container, or can be frozen.

VARIATIONS

Sponge Cake (Genoise simple)
Omit butter from genoise.

Chocolate Genoise (Genoise au chocolat)
Substitute 1 oz/30 g cocoa powder for 1 oz/30 g flour, and omit vanilla.
Coffee Genoise (Genoise au café)
Dissolve 2 tablespoons dry instant coffee in 2 tablespoons hot water and substitute for butter in genoise batter.

COFFEE GATEAU

GATEAU MOKA

The almonds coating coffee gâteau should be lightly toasted to the colour of creamy coffee.

SERVES 8

For genoise

3 oz/90 g plain flour

pinch of salt

1 ½ oz/45 g unsalted butter

3 eggs

3 oz/90 g caster sugar

few drops vanilla essence

For coffee butter cream

3 ¼ oz/100 g caster sugar

6 tablespoons water

4 egg yolks

8 oz/250 g unsalted butter

2 tablespoons dry instant coffee, dissolved in 2 tablespoons hot water

*4 fl oz/125 ml sugar syrup**

2 tablespoons rum

*4 oz/125 g sliced almonds, toasted**

powdered sugar (for sprinkling)

9 in/23 cm sloping-sided cake tin*
pastry bag* and medium star tube*

Make genoise (p. 72), bake in the cake tin and let cool. Make coffee butter cream (p. 77). Split cake horizontally and sprinkle cut sides with sugar syrup and rum. Sandwich cake with a thin layer of

butter cream and set it on a round of cardboard. Using a metal spatula, coat top and sides of cake with butter cream.

Press toasted almonds over top and sides of cake. Lay 3-4 1 in/2.5 cm bands of paper on top of cake and sprinkle generously with powdered sugar. Lift off bands, leaving a striped pattern.

Fill the pastry bag with remaining butter cream and pipe* rosettes around top edge of cake. Chill for at least 1 hour before serving.

GETTING AHEAD

Genoise, butter cream, toasted almonds and syrup can be prepared up to 3 days ahead. Assemble cake not more than a day before serving.

VARIATIONS

Chocolate Mousse Gâteau
(Gâteau à la mousse au chocolat)
Make chocolate genoise (p. 73) instead of plain genoise, and substitute chocolate mousse (p. 18) for coffee butter cream. Omit toasted almonds. Top edge of cake with rosettes of Chantilly cream* made with 4 fl oz/125 ml double cream, and decorate with chocolate rectangles* set upright around sides of cake.
Orange Gâteau (Gâteau à l'orange)
Moisten genoise with orange juice instead of sugar syrup, and Grand Marnier instead of rum. Substitute orange butter cream (p. 77) for coffee butter cream. Top edge of cake with rosettes of butter cream and candied orange julienne*.

Almond Cake

PAIN DE GENES

The almonds of Genoa have long been famous, hence the name of this rich cake. Breaking the usual rule, the ground almonds are thoroughly beaten to develop their oil.

SERVES 6-8

2 oz/60 g unsalted butter
2 ½ oz/75 g cornflour
½ teaspoon baking powder
5 oz/150 g caster sugar
5 oz/150 g ground almonds
3 eggs
1 tablespoon Kirsch (optional)
powdered sugar (for sprinkling)

10 in/25 cm sloping-sided cake tin*

Butter the cake tin, line base with a round of greaseproof paper and butter the paper. Sprinkle tin with flour and discard the excess. Melt butter and let cool. Sift cornflour with baking powder. Heat oven to gas 4/350°F/180°C.

In an electric mixer, combine sugar and ground almonds. Add eggs, one at a time, beating well after each addition until mixture is thick and creamy and holds a ribbon trail*, 6-8 minutes. Stir in Kirsch if using. Sift in cornflour and baking powder and fold* together as lightly as possible. Add melted butter just before batter is well mixed.

Pour batter into tin and bake until cake is done*, 30-35 minutes. Run a knife around the edge, turn cake out on to a rack to cool and remove paper. Sprinkle with powdered sugar just before serving.

GETTING AHEAD

Almond cake keeps well for up to a week in an airtight container, or can be frozen.

Madeleines with Honey

MADELEINES AU MIEL

The shape of madeleines is characteristic: baked in a shell-shaped mould at a high temperature, they develop a little peak on top.

MAKES 24

4 oz/125 g plain flour
1 teaspoon baking powder
4 oz/125 g unsalted butter
1 oz/30 g honey
3 eggs
3 ¼ oz/100 g caster sugar
few drops vanilla essence

24 medium madeleine moulds*

Sift flour with baking powder. Melt butter with honey and leave to cool. Whip eggs and sugar* until light, 3-4 minutes. *Note*: eggs and sugar are not whipped to a ribbon trail* as this will make the madeleines dry. Stir in vanilla essence, then fold* in flour and baking powder. Pour honey mixture over batter and fold in. Chill batter for 20-30 minutes.

Heat oven to gas 8/450°F/230°C and thoroughly butter the moulds. Using a large spoon, pour batter into moulds, filling them three-quarters full. Bake madeleines for 5 minutes. Reduce oven temperature to gas 6/400°F/200°C and continue baking until golden brown, 5-7 minutes more. Transfer them to a rack to cool.

GETTING AHEAD

Madeleines are best eaten the day of baking, though they can be stored for up to 2-3 days in an airtight container.

VARIATION

Lemon Madeleines (Madeleines au citron)
Add the grated zest of 2 lemons before folding in flour.

CHOCOLATE ROULADE WITH MINT

ROULADE AU CHOCOLAT A LA MENTHE

Chocolate and mint are natural partners.

SERVES 6-8

For chocolate genoise

1 oz/30 plain flour

¾ oz/20 g cocoa powder

½ teaspoon salt

3 eggs

3 ¼ oz/100 g caster sugar

½ teaspoon peppermint essence

3 tablespoons crème de menthe liqueur

For chocolate ganache*

4 oz/125 g plain chocolate

4 fl oz/125 ml double cream

To decorate

Chantilly cream, made with 4 fl oz/125 ml double cream*

5-6 sprigs of mint

---

pastry bag* and medium star tube*

Butter a baking sheet*, line it with greaseproof paper and butter the paper. Heat oven to gas 7/425°F/220°C.

Sift flour and coca powder with salt. Put eggs and sugar in a bowl, whip* until a ribbon trail* is formed, then stir in peppermint essence. Sift flour and cocoa over egg mixture and fold* in as lightly as possible. Spread batter evenly on baking sheet in a 10 × 16 in/25 × 40 cm rectangle. Bake until batter is risen and firm to the touch, 8-12 minutes. *Note*: do not overbake or cake will crack when rolled.

Slide cake off baking sheet on to a rack and then invert cake on to a tea towel. Remove the paper and roll up warm cake with the towel, long side inwards; then leave to cool.

Beat crème de menthe into chocolate ganache. Unroll cooled cake and trim inside edges. Spread chocolate filling on cake, reserving 3-4 tablespoons, and roll it up, using towel to roll evenly. With seam side down, trim ends diagonally and cover ends with remaining ganache.

To decorate: using the pastry bag, pipe* a line of rosettes of Chantilly cream lengthways across the top of the roll. Decorate with mint sprigs.

GETTING AHEAD

Chocolate roulade can be kept for up to 12 hours in the refrigerator, tightly covered. Decorate with Chantilly cream and add mint sprigs just before serving.

VARIATIONS

Chocolate Roulade with Orange
(Roulade au chocolat à l'orange)
Omit peppermint essence from chocolate genoise, and flavour ganache filling with Grand Marnier instead of crème de menthe. Remove peel and skin from 3 oranges and cut out segments, discarding the membranes and reserving juices to moisten cake. Spread cake with chocolate filling and top with orange segments. Instead of mint sprigs, top Chantilly cream rosettes with candied orange julienne* or thin slices of orange, halved and twisted into butterflies.

Mocha Roulade (Roulade au moka)
Make coffee genoise (p. 73) and bake as for chocolate genoise. Omit crème de menthe from filling. Top Chantilly cream rosettes with chocolate discs* instead of mint sprigs.

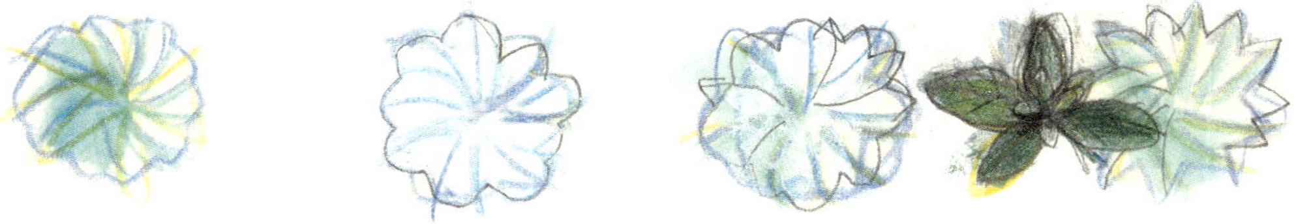

Savoy Sponge Cake

BISCUIT DE SAVOIE

A light, slightly dry cake that is excellent with tea or a glass of wine.

SERVES 8

2 oz/60 g almond sticks	*4 eggs, separated*
2 oz/60 g plain flour	*5 oz/150 g caster sugar*
2 oz/60 g potato flour	*grated zest of 1 lemon*
pinch of salt	*powdered sugar (for sprinkling)*
1 oz/30 g unsalted butter	

10 in/25 cm sloping-sided cake tin*
or 8 in/20 cm brioche mould*

Butter the cake tin or mould, line base with a round of greaseproof paper and butter paper. Sprinkle tin with flour, discarding the excess, then sprinkle with half the almond sticks. Heat oven to gas 4/350°F/180°C.

Sift flour, potato flour and salt. Melt butter and let cool. Beat egg yolks and two-thirds of sugar until light and thick, 4-5 minutes. Beat in lemon zest. Stiffly whip egg whites*, add remaining sugar and continue beating, about 30 seconds. Fold* flour and egg whites into egg yolk mixture alternately in 3 batches. Add melted butter when last batch is almost mixed. *Note*: batter will lose volume quickly after butter is added.

Pour batter into cake tin, sprinkle remaining almonds on top and bake until cake is done*, 35-40 minutes. Run a knife around the edge, turn cake out on to a rack to cool and remove paper. Sprinkle with powdered sugar before serving.

GETTING AHEAD

Savoy sponge cake is best the day it is baked but can be kept for up to 2 days in an airtight container.

VARIATIONS

Savoy Sponge Cake with Currants
(Gâteau de Savoie aux raisins de Corinthe)
When making cake batter, mix 2½ oz/75 g currants with 1 tablespoon flour. Fold into batter with last batch of flour.

Savoy Sponge Cake with Lemon
(Gâteau de Savoie au citron)
Omit almonds and top cake with lemon icing: with a vegetable peeler remove zest of 1 lemon and cut into the finest possible julienne strips*. Blanch by boiling in water for 2 minutes and draining. Make glacé icing* with 6½ oz/200 g powdered sugar and use lemon juice instead of water. Stir in lemon julienne and pour icing over cake, allowing it to drip down the sides.

Vanilla Butter Cream

CREME AU BEURRE A LA VANILLE

The richest of all fillings for cakes and petits fours. Often this basic recipe is lightened by folding in an equal volume of pastry cream.

MAKES 12 oz/375 g

3¼ oz/100 g caster sugar	*4 egg yolks*
6 tablespoons water	*8 oz/250 g unsalted butter*
	few drops vanilla essence

In a small heavy saucepan heat sugar with water until dissolved, then boil until sugar syrup* reaches soft-ball stage, 239°F/115°C on a sugar thermometer. Remove from heat and let bubbles subside.

Meanwhile, in a medium bowl beat egg yolks just until mixed. Gradually pour in hot syrup, beating constantly. *Note*: if using an electic beater, pour syrup in a thin stream between beaters so syrup does not stick to bowl. Beat as fast as possible until mixture is thick and cool.

Cream butter and gradually beat into cool yolk mixture. *Note*: if yolk mixture is warm it will melt butter. Beat in vanilla essence.

GETTING AHEAD

Butter cream can be kept for up to a week in the refrigerator, or can be frozen. On standing it solidifies, so let it come to room temperature for 1-2 hours before using, or soften it in a warm water bath*.

VARIATIONS

Chocolate Butter Cream
(Crème au beurre au chocolat)
Melt 6 oz/180 g plain chocolate, chopped, on a heatproof plate over a pan of hot water. Cool slightly and beat into vanilla butter cream.

Coffee Butter Cream (Crème au beurre au café)
Dissolve 2 tablespoons dry instant coffee in 2 tablespoons hot water and beat into vanilla butter cream.

Light Butter Cream (Crème au beurre légère)
Beat half quantity of vanilla pastry cream (p. 58) into vanilla butter cream. Add flavourings as in other variations.

Orange Butter Cream (Crème au beurre à l'orange)
Beat the grated zest of 2 oranges, 4 tablespoons orange juice and 3 tablespoons Grand Marnier into vanilla butter cream.

Praline Butter Cream (Crème au beurre pralinée)
Beat praline* made with 3 oz/90 g whole unblanched almonds into vanilla butter cream.

Raspberry Butter Cream
(Crème au beurre à la framboise)
Purée 8 oz/250 g fresh or frozen raspberries in a blender or food processor. Strain to remove seeds and beat into vanilla butter cream.

BRETON BUTTER CAKE

GATEAU BRETON

Good butter gives all the flavour needed to this extraordinarily rich gâteau, a cross between a pound cake and a biscuit.

SERVES 8

8 oz/250 g plain flour	*8 oz/250 g caster sugar*
8 oz/250 g butter, cut into small pieces	*6 egg yolks*

9-10 in/23-25 cm tart tin with removable base*

Heat oven to gas 5/375°F/190°C and butter the tin.

Sift flour on to a work surface and make a large well in the centre. Add pieces of butter to well with sugar and egg yolks, reserving a teaspoon of egg yolk for glaze. Work together with your fingertips until smooth. Gradually draw in flour, using fingers and heel of your hand, then work dough until smooth. It will be sticky and must be mixed with the help of a pastry scraper or metal spatula.

Spread mixture in tin and smooth the top, flouring the back of your hand to prevent sticking. Brush surface of gâteau with reserved egg yolk and mark a lattice pattern with the tines of a fork.

Bake for 20 minutes. Reduce oven temperature to gas 4/350°F/180°C and continue baking until cake is golden and firm to the touch, about 30 minutes.

Leave to cool, then unmould carefully on to a rack.

GETTING AHEAD

Breton butter cake can be stored for up to 2 weeks in an airtight container, and the flavour mellows on keeping.

Pineapple Gateau

GATEAU ANANAS

Symbol of fertility, the shape of a pineapple is traced in meringue on top of this cake, giving a clue to the pineapple filling.

SERVES 8-10

For genoise

4 oz/125 g plain flour

pinch of salt

2 oz/60 g unsalted butter

4 eggs

4 oz/125 g caster sugar

few drops vanilla essence

For Italian meringue

6 oz/180 g caster sugar

3 fl oz/75 ml water

3 egg whites

few drops vanilla essence

For vanilla pastry cream

8 fl oz/250 ml milk

1 vanilla pod or few drops vanilla essence

3 egg yolks

1¾ oz/50 g caster sugar

⅓ oz/12 g plain flour

For filling

1 small fresh pineapple, peeled, core discarded and chopped or 1 lb/500 g canned pineapple chunks in light syrup, drained, chopped and juice reserved

2 tablespoons Kirsch

Chantilly cream, made with 4 fl oz/125 ml double cream*

To decorate

*4 fl oz/125 ml apricot jam glaze**

few strips angelica

8 in/20 cm square cake tin*
pastry bag* and small star tube*

Make genoise (p. 72), bake in the cake tin and let cool. Make Italian meringue (p. 82).

For filling: make vanilla pastry cream (p. 58), stir in chopped pineapple and Kirsch and then fold* in Chantilly cream.

Split cake into 3 layers horizontally and sprinkle with any juice from fresh pineapple, or reserved juice from canned pineapple. Set on a sheet of cardboard and sandwich cake layers with filling. Heat oven to gas 7/425°F/220°C.

Smoothly coat sides of cake with Italian meringue, using a metal spatula. Fill the pastry bag with remaining meringue and pipe* small rosettes to completely coat top of cake, leaving a large oval diagonally across the centre to represent the pineapple. Pipe* a border of rosettes around base of cake.

Bake gâteau until meringue points are toasted, 4-5 minutes. To decorate: melt apricot glaze and spoon into pineapple shape. Add strips of angelica at one end of pineapple to represent leaves. Transfer gâteau to a serving plate and keep in refrigerator.

GETTING AHEAD

Genoise, pineapple and pastry cream filling can be kept for up to 24 hours in the refrigerator. Pineapple and Chantilly cream must not be added to pastry cream nor gâteau completed more than 2 hours before serving.

VARIATION

Strawberry Gâteau (Gâteau aux fraises)
Substitute sliced fresh strawberries for pineapple in filling. Pipe* meringue, leaving a heart shape to represent a strawberry, and fill with melted strawberry jelly instead of apricot glaze.

CHOCOLATE CHEQUER BOARD

DAMIER AU CHOCOLAT

This apparently plain chocolate cake reveals a chequered effect when sliced.

SERVES 10

12 oz/375 g plain flour
1 ½ tablespoons baking powder
1 ½ oz/45 g cocoa powder
2 oz/60 g unsalted butter
10 oz/300 g caster sugar
6 eggs
few drops vanilla essence
*4 fl oz/125 ml sugar syrup**
2-3 tablespoons brandy or rum (optional)

To finish

*4 oz/125 g apricot jam glaze**

For chocolate ganache*

8 oz/250 g plain chocolate
8 fl oz/250 ml double cream

three 9 in/23 cm cake tins* 1-1½ in/2.5-4 cm deep
2 pastry bags* and two ½ in/1 cm plain tubes*

Butter the cake tins, line bases with rounds of greaseproof paper and butter the paper. Sprinkle tins with flour, discarding the excess. Heat oven to gas 4/350°F/180°C.

Sift half the flour with half the baking powder and set aside. In another bowl, sift together the remaining flour, cocoa and remaining baking powder. Cream butter and sugar until light and soft, 4-5 minutes. Add eggs, one at a time, beating until mixture is smooth and creamy after each addition. Stir in vanilla essence. Divide batter in half and fold* cocoa mixture into one portion and plain flour mixture into the other.

Fill one pastry bag with chocolate mixture and the other with plain. Pipe* a ring of chocolate batter around the edge of one cake tin. Pipe a round of plain batter inside the chocolate ring. Continue alternating rings of batter until tin is full. Fill remaining tins in the same way, starting with a ring of plain batter in one tin.

Bake cakes until they are done*, 20-25 minutes. Run a knife around the sides and turn cakes out on to a rack to cool, discarding paper. While still warm, sprinkle them with sugar syrup and brandy or rum if using.

To finish: melt apricot glaze. Brush it on the cake layers and pile one on another, with plain outer ring in the centre. Set cake on a round of cardboard. Spread top and sides of cake with chocolate ganache, making decorative swirls with a metal spatula. Chill for at least 2 hours.

GETTING AHEAD

Chequer board can be kept for up to 3 days in the refrigerator.

VARIATION

Raspberry Chequer Board (Damier aux framboises) Omit cocoa powder and colour half of mixture with few drops red food colouring to make a light pink batter. Substitute raspberry jelly or jam for apricot. Coat cake with raspberry butter cream (p. 77), reserving some for decoration. Cover top of cake completely with 12 oz/375 g fresh raspberries and brush with 8 fl oz/250 ml redcurrant jelly glaze*. Decorate edge of cake with rosettes of reserved butter cream.

—10— MERINGUES

I was once admonished as a teenager, "The test of a lady is the ability to eat a meringue gracefully." For several formal afternoon teas after that I tried my best to appear sophisticated, but greed invariably won. For who could resist the puffy clouds of home-made meringue sandwiched with Chantilly cream that adorned the table?

I later learned that a romance with meringue could extend to *vacherin* meringue cases filled with whipped cream and fruit or ice-cream. In France I made the acquaintance of the classic trio of almond and hazelnut gâteaux *Dacquoise*, *Progrès* and *Succès*, each sandwiched with various flavours of butter cream and left to mellow to a crisp and creamy blend. With a French family I came across snow eggs of poached meringue floating in a bowl of egg custard and topped with caramel, an ideal end to a festive lunch.

How like the French to take a basic (and inexpensive) preparation like meringue and transform it in so many different ways. There are even several methods of preparing meringue itself, two of which are given here – Swiss meringue, made of egg whites and caster sugar, and Italian meringue, where the sugar is cooked to syrup before adding to the whites. Fluffier than Italian meringue, Swiss meringue is used for plain meringues, meringue cases, and for toppings. It should be baked at once for on standing the sugar dissolves to syrup in the whites.

Italian meringue, on the other hand, holds up well because the egg whites are cooked by the scalding sugar syrup. Pastry shops keep a supply of it on hand for sweetening cream, for lightening pastry cream and sorbets and to use as a basic part of butter cream. With its stiffer texture, Italian meringue is easy to pipe and in the oven it bakes quite hard. It is used for petits fours and for mounting Swiss meringue shapes together to make *vacherin* and meringue baskets.

To make best use of meringue, a pastry bag is essential in shaping the circles, rosettes and whirls which are almost as appealing as its delicate cream colour. Meringue should never brown. It is cooked at a very low temperature so that it dries rather than bakes. If it does brown too much, all is not lost, for a coating of cream hides a multitude of sins. If it should stick to the baking sheet and crack, crushed meringue layered with fruit and cream is a face-saving treat.

KEYS TO THE BEST MERINGUES

Be sure the egg whites are at room temperature and whip them very stiff before adding sugar.

For detailed instructions on whipping egg whites see Glossary pp. 88-92.

After adding all the sugar for Swiss meringue, continue beating just long enough for the sugar to dissolve a little so the meringue forms long peaks when the whisk is lifted. It should be stiff enough to pipe. If not beaten long enough, Swiss meringue loses shape and separates slightly in the oven. If overbeaten, however, the sugar forms syrup and the meringue "weeps".

For Italian meringue, boil the sugar syrup exactly to the hard-ball stage (120°C/248°F on a sugar thermometer). If the syrup is too thin, the meringue will not be stiff; if too concentrated, it crystallizes rather than mixing with the egg whites.

When piping, large tubes are needed for Swiss meringue so as not to crush the mixture, but Italian meringue is firm enough to pipe in quite small, intricate patterns.

Meringue sticks easily during baking so baking sheets must be thoroughly buttered, then chilled to set the butter before sprinkling flour. Alternatively you can use non-stick silicone coated paper or a non-stick baking sheet.

A sprinkling of caster sugar before baking gives Swiss meringue a shiny, crisp surface. Italian meringue, however, is already shiny with cooked sugar.

Meringue must be baked in a very low oven but at these temperatures a thermostat is often inaccurate, so keep a close watch. If it starts to colour, lower the oven temperature and if necessary open the door for a few minutes.

Cooking times are very approximate. Long slow cooking is the aim so that the meringue dries thoroughly.

When cooked, meringue will be firm to the touch, but it may not be crisp until it cools.

The texture of meringue containing nuts will be quite soft, particularly after keeping, and some people like a slightly sticky underdone centre for plain meringues too.

Meringues keep perfectly for weeks in an airtight container and they can be frozen. Once a filling is added, however, they soften within a few hours.

Sometimes gâteaux, particularly those with nuts, are deliberately kept for a day or two so that they moisten and mellow.

ITALIAN MERINGUE

MERINGUE ITALIENNE

A close-textured meringue which is easy to pipe.

MAKES TWELVE 3 in/7 cm MERINGUES

8 oz/250 g caster sugar | *4 egg whites*
4 fl oz/125 ml water | *few drops vanilla essence*

Heat sugar with water over a low heat until dissolved. Bring to the boil and boil without stirring until sugar syrup* reaches the hard-ball stage (248°F/120°C on a sugar thermometer). Let bubbles subside.

Meanwhile, stiffly whip egg whites*. Gradually pour in hot syrup, beating constantly.

Note: if using an electric beater, pour syrup in a thin stream between beaters so syrup does not stick to bowl.

Continue beating until meringue is cold. Stir in vanilla essence.

GETTING AHEAD

Italian meringue can be kept for up to a week in the refrigerator, tightly covered.

Swiss Meringue

MERINGUE SUISSE

The fluffiest type of meringue.

MAKES TWELVE 3 in/7 cm MERINGUES

4 egg whites
8 oz/250 g caster sugar
few drops vanilla essence

Stiffly whip egg whites*. Add 4 tablespoons of sugar and continue beating until egg whites are glossy, ½-1 minute. Fold* in remaining sugar, a few tablespoons at a time, and continue folding until meringue forms long peaks when the whisk is lifted, ½-1 minute. *Note*: do not overmix or the sugar will dissolve and the meringue will become liquid. Stir in vanilla essence.

GETTING AHEAD

Swiss meringue can be kept for up to an hour in the refrigerator, covered with a damp cloth. If kept too long the sugar melts.

Chantilly Meringues

MERINGUES CHANTILLY

Shaping plain meringues with 2 spoons is traditional, but piping the mixture gives a professional look.

MAKES 10

For Swiss meringue
4 egg whites
8 oz/250 g caster sugar
few drops vanilla essence

caster sugar (for sprinkling)
Chantilly cream, made with 8 fl oz/250 ml double cream*

---

pastry bag* and large star tube* (optional)

Heat oven to gas ½/250°F/120°C. Butter and flour a baking sheet*, shaking off excess, or use non-stick paper or non-stick baking sheets. Make Swiss meringue (p. 83). Using the pastry bag, pipe* 3 in/7 cm mounds of meringue on baking sheet. Alternatively, shape meringue into ovals using 2 tablespoons.

Sprinkle meringues generously with sugar and bake until firm to the touch, about 1 hour. Lift meringues off the baking sheet with a sharp knife and press the bottoms gently, to collapse them and form a hollow. Continue baking until shells are crisp, ½-1 hour more.

To finish: using the pastry bag, pipe* large rosettes of Chantilly cream on underside of half the meringues. Add second meringue to each at an angle, so the cream puffs out.

GETTING AHEAD

Meringues can be kept for up to 2-3 weeks in an airtight container. Add cream not more than 2 hours before serving.

VARIATIONS

Chocolate Chantilly Meringues

(Meringues Chantilly au chocolat)
Fold 1 oz/30 g cocoa powder into Swiss meringue. Dust meringues with cocoa powder instead of caster sugar.
Ice-cream Meringues (Meringues à la glace)
Omit Chantilly cream. Fill meringues with vanilla, chocolate or strawberry ice-cream (pp. 36 or 38) and serve at once.

COFFEE ALMOND MERINGUE GATEAU

DACQUOISE AU CAFE

A gâteau from Dax in the Pyrenees.

SERVES 6-8

For Swiss meringue
4 egg whites
8 oz/250 g caster sugar
few drops vanilla essence
4 oz/125 g ground almonds
2 tablespoons cornflour
caster sugar (for sprinkling)

For coffee butter cream
5 oz/150 g caster sugar
8 tablespoons water
6 egg yolks
12 oz/375 g unsalted butter
3 tablespoons dry instant coffee, dissolved in
3 tablespoons hot water
2 oz/60 g toasted chopped almonds*

pastry bag*
small star tube* and ½ in/1 cm plain tube*

Heat oven to gas ½/250°F/120°C. Butter and flour a baking sheet*, shaking off excess flour. Mark two 8 in/20 cm circles with a pan lid or flan ring on the sheet. Alternatively, line baking sheet with non-stick silicone paper, drawing circles with a pencil.

Make Swiss meringue (p. 83). Fold* in ground almonds and cornflour. Using the pastry bag with plain tube, pipe* spirals of meringue to form rounds, starting at the outside edge and working inwards. Alternatively, spread meringue into rounds with a metal spatula. Sprinkle meringue generously with caster sugar and bake until firm to the touch and lightly coloured, about 1 hour. Let meringues cool slightly, then transfer to a rack to cool completely.

Make coffee butter cream (p. 77). Sandwich meringues and coat sides of gâteau with butter cream, reserving 10-12 tablespoons. Press chopped almonds around sides of gâteau and, using the pastry bag and small star tube, pipe* small rosettes of butter cream to completely cover the top. Keep for at least a day so that meringue softens and flavour of gâteau mellows.

GETTING AHEAD

Coffee almond meringue gâteau can be stored for up to 3 days in the refrigerator, or can be frozen.

VARIATIONS

Almond and Hazelnut Meringue Gâteau
(Gâteau Progrès)
Substitute 2 oz/60 g toasted* ground hazelnuts for half ground almonds in meringue. Reduce coffee butter cream to 1 recipe (p. 77), substituting 1 recipe praline butter cream (p. 77) for omitted coffee butter cream. Omit rosettes and sprinkle top thickly with powdered sugar. Pipe* the word "Progrès" across the top with butter cream, using a ¼ in/5 mm plain tube.
Almond and Pistachio Meringue Gâteau
(Gâteau Succès)
Reduce coffee butter cream to 1 recipe (p. 77). Omit rosettes and generously sprinkle top of gâteau with cocoa powder. Substitute finely chopped blanched* pistachios for almonds around the sides, and pipe* the word "Succès" across the top using a ¼ in/5 mm plain tube.
Grand Marnier Meringue Gâteau
(Dacquoise au Grand Marnier)
Substitute 1½ recipe orange butter cream (p. 77) for coffee butter cream.

Meringue Basket with Fruits

VACHERIN AUX FRUITS

So that the meringue is crisp right through, a *vacherin* is constructed in 2 stages. First the base and sides of Swiss meringue are baked, then these pieces are mounted with more meringue into a basket which is baked again. For filling, choose colourful fruits such as strawberries, raspberries or cherries.

SERVES 10-12

For Swiss meringue

3 egg whites

6 oz/180 g caster sugar

few drops vanilla essence

caster sugar (for sprinkling)

For Italian meringue

6 oz/180 g caster sugar

4 fl oz/125 ml water

3 egg whites

few drops vanilla essence

For filling

1 ½ lb/750 g fresh berries, hulled and washed only if sandy

2-3 tablespoons caster sugar

2-3 tablespoons Grand Marnier

Chantilly cream, made with 12 fl oz/350 ml double cream*

---

pastry bag*
¾ in/2 cm plain tube*
medium and large star tubes*

Heat oven to gas ½/250°F/120°C. Butter and flour 2 baking sheets*, shaking off excess flour. Mark an 8 in/20 cm circle on one sheet with a pan lid or flan ring. Alternatively, line baking sheet with non-stick silicone paper, drawing circle with a pencil.

Make Swiss meringue (p. 83). Using the pastry bag with plain tube, pipe* a round of meringue, starting at the outside edge of the marked circle and working inwards. Pipe remaining meringue on to second sheet, in strips that are 3 in/7 cm long and 1½ in/4 cm wide. There should be about 20 individual meringues. Sprinkle meringues generously with caster sugar and bake until firm to the touch, about 1 hour. *Note*: do not allow them to colour.

Make Italian meringue (p. 82), or a second batch of Swiss meringue (p. 83). Using the pastry bag and medium star tube, pipe* a generous ring of rosettes at edge of meringue round. Mount individual meringues upright in the rosettes as sides of the basket, piping meringue between them to glue them together. Decorate outside of *vacherin* with rosettes of remaining meringue and continue baking in the oven until whole *vacherin* is firm and light golden, ¾-1 hour. Transfer *vacherin* to a rack to cool.

For filling: sprinkle berries with sugar and liqueur and leave for a few minutes to macerate. Pile half the Chantilly cream inside *vacherin* and top with fruit. Fill pastry bag with remaining Chantilly cream, using the large star tube, and pipe* rosettes to completely cover fruit. Chill until serving.

To serve: cut *vacherin* in wedges like a cake, using a sharp knife.

GETTING AHEAD

The meringue shell can be kept for up to 2-3 weeks in an airtight container. Fill it not more than 2 hours before serving.

VARIATION

Small Meringue Boats with Fruit
(Barquettes meringuées aux fruits)
Omit Italian meringue. Using a ⅜ in/1 cm plain tube, pipe* half the Swiss meringue into 10-12 ovals and 10-12 rings of the same size and bake for 4-5 minutes. Fill pastry bag with remaining meringue and, using small star tube, mount baked rings on ovals. Cover sides completely with rosettes. Reduce fruit quantity to 8 oz/250 g and make Chantilly cream with 6 fl oz/175 ml double cream. Fill boats with fruits and cream and decorate.

Meringues with Chestnut and Whipped Cream

MONT BLANCS

Inspired by France's highest mountain.

SERVES 10

For Swiss meringue

4 egg whites

8 oz/250 g caster sugar

few drops vanilla essence

For topping

*2 lb/1 kg fresh chestnuts, peeled and cooked**, *or 1½ lb/750 g canned chestnuts in water*

*8 fl oz/250 ml sugar syrup**, *more if needed*

*Chantilly cream**, *made with 12 fl oz/350 ml double cream*

1 oz/30 g plain chocolate, grated

pastry bag*
¼ in/5 mm and ½ in/1 cm plain tubes*

Heat oven to gas ½/250°F/120°C. Butter and flour 2 baking sheets*, shaking off excess flour. Mark ten 4 in/10 cm circles on sheets with a pan lid or pastry cutter. Alternatively, line baking sheets with non-stick silicone paper, drawing circles with a pencil.

Make Swiss meringue (p. 83). Using the pastry bag and larger plain tube, pipe* spirals of meringue in circles to form rounds. Sprinkle generously with sugar and bake until firm to the touch, about 1 hour. *Note*: the meringue should not colour. Let meringues cool slightly, then transfer to a rack to cool completely.

Drain cooked fresh or canned chestnuts and purée* them. Stir enough sugar syrup into chestnut purée to make it thin enough to pipe. *Note*: purée is heavy if too much syrup is added. Using the pastry bag and smaller tube, pipe* rough mounds of purée on to the meringue rounds. Top each with peaks of Chantilly cream and sprinkle with grated chocolate. Chill until serving.

GETTING AHEAD

The meringue can be baked and the chestnut purée prepared up to 2 days ahead. Keep meringue in an airtight container and the purée in the refrigerator. Make Chantilly cream and assemble Mont Blancs not more than 2 hours before serving.

VARIATIONS

Large Meringue with Chestnuts and Whipped Cream (Grand Mont Blanc)
Make 2 large gâteaux instead of 10 small ones.

Birds' Nests (Nids d'oiseaux)
Pipe* chestnut purée around the edge of the cooked meringue rounds to resemble bird nests. Fill the centres with cream and top each with 3-4 small chocolate eggs or chocolate discs*.

Snow Eggs

OEUFS A LA NEIGE

A classic which is popular with all generations.

SERVES 6-8

For vanilla custard sauce

1 pt/600 ml milk

1 vanilla pod

6 egg yolks

1 ½ oz/45 g caster sugar

For Swiss meringue

4 egg whites

8 oz/250 g caster sugar

few drops vanilla essence

For caramel*

3 ¼ oz/100 g caster sugar

pastry bag* and large star tube* (optional)

In a wide shallow pan, gently heat milk for custard. Make Swiss meringue (p. 83). If using a pastry bag, pipe* large "eggs" of meringue on to a buttered baking sheet, then drop them into hot milk. Alternatively, shape meringue with 2 tablespoons and drop "eggs" directly into milk. Poach "eggs", a few at a time, in milk until firm and slightly puffed, 4-5 minutes. Turn them once during poaching. Drain them on paper towels and poach remaining "eggs".

Strain poaching milk and make vanilla custard sauce (p. 33). Strain into a shallow serving bowl and let cool. Pile meringue eggs into the cooled custard. Make caramel (p. 88), let bubbles subside and trail it over the eggs in a lattice pattern. Serve chilled.

GETTING AHEAD

Eggs and custard can be kept for up to 12 hours in the refrigerator, tightly covered. Add caramel not more than an hour before serving.

VARIATIONS

Chocolate Snow Eggs (Oeufs à la neige au chocolat)

Substitute chocolate custard sauce (p. 33) for vanilla custard sauce. Omit caramel and sprinkle eggs with 1 oz/30 g plain chocolate, grated, or ½ recipe chocolate sauce (p. 32), cooked until quite thick.

Almond Snow Eggs (Oeufs à la neige aux amandes) Sprinkle eggs and custard with 2 oz/60 g toasted* sliced almonds.

GLOSSARY

Baking Blind
Baking blind means to cook an empty pastry shell before a filling is added.

Line* a tart or tartlet tin* with pastry dough and chill until very firm, for at least 15 minutes. Heat oven to gas 7/425°F/220°C. Cut a circle of greaseproof paper or foil 2 in/5 cm larger than the diameter of the tart or tartlet tin. Crumple the paper and line the pastry with it, pressing well into the corners. Fill paper three-quarters full with dried beans or rice to hold dough in shape.

To cook a tart: bake for 10 minutes, reduce oven temperature to gas 5/375°F/190°C and continue baking until the pastry is set and lightly browned, about 5 minutes. Remove paper and beans and bake the tart shell until browned, 8-12 minutes more.

To cook tartlets: bake for 10 minutes, remove paper and beans and continue cooking until browned, 3-8 minutes more.

Baking Sheets
Baking sheets should be thick so that they do not warp. Common materials include the traditional steel, which conducts heat well, and aluminium, which is light to handle. For meringues and petits fours, a non-stick finish is helpful. To discourage sticking, do not wash baking sheets but, while still warm, rub them clean with a rough cloth. In the oven, the edges of the sheet should not touch the sides, so as to allow air to circulate freely.

Balloon whisk, see *Whisks and Electric Mixers*
Brioche tins, see *Tins*
Cake tins, see *Tins*

Cakes, Testing When Done
When a cake shrinks slightly from the sides of the tin, it is probably done. For sponge mixtures, press the top lightly with your finger – the cake should feel firm and the mark should disappear. For heavier batters, insert a toothpick or skewer in the centre of the cake – if it is clean when withdrawn, the cake is done.

Candied Citrus Julienne
For candied zest of 2 oranges, 4 lemons or 4 limes: thinly pare zest from fruit using a vegetable peeler. Cut zest into the thinnest possible julienne strips with a sharp knife. Put them in a small pan with 1 oz/30 g caster sugar and 2 tablespoons water. Heat gently until sugar is dissolved, then simmer until all water has evaporated and julienne is very tender and looks transparent, 8-10 minutes.

Candied Citrus Slices
For candied slices of 1 orange, 2 lemons or 2 limes: slice fruit, including peel, about ⅛ in/3 mm thick and arrange in a large frying pan so that all slices touch the bottom. Sprinkle with ½ oz/15 g caster sugar, turn over and sprinkle other side with same amount of sugar. Pour over 2 tablespoons water and cook slices very gently, turning occasionally, until they are tender and look transparent, 10-15 minutes. *Note*: do not allow slices to caramelize. If water evaporates too quickly during cooking, add more.

Caramel
For caramel made with 3¼ oz/100 g caster sugar: in a heavy-bottomed pan, heat sugar with 6 tablespoons water until dissolved. Boil without stirring until syrup cooks to a golden brown caramel. *Note*: the syrup starts to colour quite suddenly and will continue to cook in the heat of the pan. If it burns, it will be bitter. Take from the heat, let bubbles subside and use as stated in the recipe.

To dissolve caramel for flavouring or sauce: add 2 fl oz/60 ml water to the caramel while still hot. *Note*: stand back as it will splutter and wear an oven glove or wrap the hand holding the pan in a towel. Heat gently until caramel is dissolved.

Chantilly Cream
For Chantilly cream made with 8 fl oz/250 ml double cream: put chilled cream in a bowl over ice and water and whisk until stiff. *Note*: if cream is not cold it may curdle before it stiffens. Add 1-2 tablespoons caster sugar to taste, with few drops vanilla essence, and continue whisking until cream stiffens again. *Note*: do not overbeat or cream will curdle. Chantilly cream can be stored in the refrigerator for up to 12 hours. It will separate slightly on standing, but will re-combine if stirred briskly.

Chestnuts: Peeling, Cooking and Puréeing
Weight for weight, canned chestnuts are the equivalent of fresh unpeeled nuts.

To peel fresh chestnuts: pierce each nut with a sharp knife. Bring them to the boil in water. Drain a few at a time and peel while still hot, removing outer and inner skin. If they cool and become hard to peel, reheat them.

To cook chestnuts: bring peeled chestnuts to the boil in water in a covered pan and simmer until tender, 30-40 minutes. Add more water if necessary during cooking to keep chestnuts covered. Drain thoroughly.

To purée chestnuts: drain fresh or canned chestnuts and purée in a food processor. Alternatively, work them through a vegetable mill.

Chocolate Decorations
For twelve to sixteen 1 in/2.5 cm decorations: melt 3 oz/90 g plain chocolate on a heatproof plate over a pan of hot water. Let it cool slightly, then spread on greaseproof paper to an even ⅛ in/3 mm layer. Chill until set.

With a sharp knife or a small round pastry cutter, cut squares, diamonds, discs, ovals etc. for decoration.

Chocolate Ganache
For ganache made with 8 oz/250 g plain chocolate: chop chocolate and melt on a heatproof plate over a pan of hot water. Bring 8 fl oz/250 ml double cream just to the boil. Take from the heat, stir in chocolate and beat until very smooth. Pour into a bowl, let cool to tepid, then whisk until light and thick.

Ganache can be stored in the refrigerator for up to a week, or can be frozen. To soften ganache to use, warm in a water bath* until melted, let cool and whisk again until thick.

Citrus Julienne
Thinly pare zest from fruit using a vegetable peeler. Pile 2-3 pieces of zest on top of each other and with a sharp chopping knife, cut the thinnest possible lengthways strips.

Copper Bowl and Whisk
The unlined copper bowls made for whipping egg whites* are hemispherical so that the whisk reaches every corner. A ring at the rim makes the bowl easy to hold and hang up for storage. Sizes vary from 10 in/25 cm for up to 8 egg whites, to 12 in/30 cm for 8-12 egg whites. In a larger bowl, the quantity of egg whites is so big as to be very hard to whisk.

A copper bowl should be used with a large balloon whisk* (recognizable by its long wooden handle) so that the maximum amount of air is beaten into the egg whites. Before using the bowl, always clean the inside by rubbing with 1-2 tablespoons coarse salt and 1-2 tablespoons vinegar (or use salt and lemon juice). Rinse and dry the bowl thoroughly; the copper should be bright and have a pinkish tone. The bowl can be cleaned an hour ahead, but not more.

Egg Glaze
Egg glaze is brushed on pastry and bread dough to give a golden gloss after baking.

With a whisk or fork beat a whole egg with a large pinch (about ½ teaspoon) salt for 1 minute until thoroughly combined. If glaze is left 5 minutes or more, the salt breaks down albumin in egg white so the glaze thins and coats more evenly.

Electric mixer, see *Whisks*

Folding Together Mixtures
Two mixtures fold together most easily if their consistency is similar. If one ingredient is much lighter than the other, first stir a little of the lighter mixture thoroughly into the heavier mixture; then add the remainder of the lighter mixture.

Using a wooden spatula or large metal spoon, cut across the centre of the mixture, scraping the bottom of the bowl and scooping the spoon under the mixture towards the left side of the bowl. At the same time, with your left hand, turn the bowl anticlockwise. This should be a synchronized movement: cut and scoop with the spatula in one hand, turn the bowl with the other. In this way, the spatula reaches the maximum volume of mixture in one movement, so that it is folded quickly and loses a minimum of air.

Frosted fruits, see *Fruits*

Fruit Glazes
For 8 fl oz/250 ml apricot glaze: in a saucepan (not aluminium) melt 12 oz/375 g apricot jam with the juice of ½ lemon and 2-3 tablespoons water. Work through a sieve to remove lumps. For coating, glaze is reheated to melt it. Glaze can be stored like jam.

For 8 fl oz/250 ml redcurrant glaze: in a saucepan (not aluminium) melt 12 oz/375 g redcurrant jelly with 1-2 tablespoons water. Stir jelly gently and do not boil or the colour will darken. Use warm. Glaze can be stored like jelly.

Fruits, Frosted
Fruits for frosting must have a thick skin so that juice does not leak; redcurrants, grapes and cherries are suitable.

For 8 oz/250 g frosted fruit: wash and dry the fruits, leaving on stalks. Whip 2 egg whites* until frothy. Dip fruits, singly or a small bunch at a time, into whipped egg whites, then into caster sugar. Set on greaseproof paper, sprinkle with more sugar and leave for about 1 hour to dry. *Note*: on a humid day, frosted fruits are hard to make. Frosted fruits can be stored for up to 4-6 hours in the refrigerator.

Fruits, Poached
For 2 lb/1 kg poached fruit: in a deep saucepan heat 6½ oz/200 g caster sugar with 1⅔ pt/1 litre water and the pared rind and juice of 2 lemons until the sugar is dissolved. Boil the syrup for 2 minutes. Prepare fruit as required in recipe, adding them at once to the syrup so that they do not discolour. The fruits should be completely immersed in syrup – if necessary, cook them in 2 batches. Poach the fruits, cooking just below the boiling point, until they are very tender and look transparent. Cooking time varies not only with the type of fruit, but with ripeness.

Gelatine
Before adding to a mixture, gelatine must be first softened and then melted. To soften, sprinkle the powdered gelatine over 2-3 tablespoons water (or other liquid as specified in the recipe) in a small saucepan. Never add the liquid to the gelatine. Melt the gelatine over low heat, stirring once or twice until it is completely melted. *Note*: do not let it boil, or it will cook into strings.

Stir the melted gelatine into a mixture while still warm; preferably the mixture is warm also. As the gelatine mixture cools, stir it from time to time, particularly if working over ice. When it is cold to the touch, it will set quite suddenly. Take it from the ice and at once fold* in any other ingredients.

Glacé Icing
For glacé icing made with 6½ oz/200 g powdered sugar: sift sugar into a small bowl and stir in 6-7 tablespoons water with a few drops vanilla essence. For a tart-flavoured icing, lemon juice can be substituted for water and vanilla. Set bowl in a water bath* and heat, stirring, until tepid. The icing should just coat the back of a spoon. If too thin, beat in more sifted, powdered sugar; if too thick, add a little more water. Use warm so that icing sets as it cools.

Glazed fruits, see *Fruits*

Hard-ball stage, see *Sugar Syrup*

Hard-crack stage, see *Sugar Syrup*

Ice-Cream Machines
The best ice-creams and sorbets are made in the new electric machines which churn the mixture at the same time as chilling it. They are quick and simple to use and come in several sizes, but they are expensive.

Traditional churns with buckets to hold ice and salt perform the same function, but they are messy and take more time to operate, even when the churn is powered by electricity.

More practical are electric churns designed to go into the freezer – a three-star freezer with low temperature setting is essential. However, the ice-cream or sorbet will not be quite as smooth as with a free-standing electric machine.

Simplest of all are the new hand-operated churns consisting of a small paddle in a low temperature container, which is first chilled in the freezer. The ice-cream or sorbet may not be of the finest quality, but these little churns are certainly easy and inexpensive.

Julienne, see *Candied Citrus* and *Citrus Julienne*

Lemon Slices and **Julienne**, see *Candied Citrus* and *Citrus Julienne*

Lining Tins
Tart tins: if possible use a tart tin with a removable base so that the finished tart can be turned out easily. Butter the tin and roll out dough to ¼ in/5 mm thickness. Wrap dough around the rolling pin, lift it over the tin and unroll it. Let dough rest over the edge of the tin, overlapping it slightly inside. Be careful not to stretch dough. Gently lift the edges of dough with one hand and press it well into the bottom corners of the tin with the other.

Roll the rolling pin over the top of the tin to cut off excess dough. Using your forefinger and thumb, press dough evenly up the sides from the bottom to increase the height of the rim. Neaten the rim with your finger and thumb and flute it if you like. Do not let dough overlap the edge of the tin. Prick the base of the shell thoroughly to prevent the formation of air bubbles during cooking and chill until firm, for at least 15 minutes, before baking.

Tartlet tins: butter the tins and arrange close together near the work surface. Roll out the dough to ¼ in/5 mm thickness. Wrap dough around the rolling pin, lift it and gently lay it on top of the tins, being careful not to stretch dough. Press dough gently into the base of the tins, using a ball of dough dipped in flour.

Roll the rolling pin over the tops of the tins to trim the pastry. Using your forefinger and thumb, press the dough evenly up the sides of the tins from the bottoms to increase the height of the edges. Neaten the edges with your finger and thumb. Do not let the dough overlap the edges of the tins. Prick the bottoms of the shells thoroughly to prevent the formation of air bubbles during cooking. Chill the tartlets until firm, 10-15 minutes, before baking.

Moulds
Metal is the most popular material for moulds as it is easy to craft

into intricate shapes. Also it conducts heat well, so fillings brown in the oven and cold mixtures are easy to unmould. To loosen a cold mixture, either wrap the mould in a towel dipped in hot water, or dip it briefly in a bowl of warm water (for ice-cream the water should be scarcely tepid). *Note*: fruit mixtures do better in china moulds as they tend to discolour if stored in metal (unless it is stainless).

Charlotte mould: these have a characteristic bucket shape so that the mixture looks impressivly tall when turned out, yet holds firm because of the sloping sides. Charlotte moulds have 2 convenient little handles and sometimes come with a lid. Their size is measured by volume, starting with individual models and ranging to 2 pt/1.2 litre sizes which serve 6-8.

Ice-cream moulds: almost any shape; a tall cone and a square with a flower pattern on the base are traditional, while moulds shaped as fruits such as melon are particularly attractive.

Kugelhopfmould: see *Ring mould*

Madeleine moulds: a pretty shell shape, these are stamped in metal sheets of 10 or 12 moulds. Most are about 3 in/7.5 cm long but tiny madeleine moulds for petits fours are also obtainable.

Peaked moulds: these come in such intricate shapes that they are a decoration in themselves. Often nothing more is needed than a ring of contrasting sauce around the base. Mixtures formed in a peaked mould must hold their shape well, however, as with for example Bavarian creams and some mousses.

Ring moulds: these are most useful of all and accommodate all sorts of hot and cold mixtures, including cakes. Ring moulds are measured by volume. Both plain (often called savarin) and fluted (Kugelhopf) types are practical; a non-stick finish helps when ring moulds are used for baking.

Savarin mould: see *Ring mould*

Nuts, Blanching

To peel almonds and pistachios, they must be blanched: put them in a pan of cold water, bring to a boil and simmer 1 minute. Drain, rinse with cold water and peel.

Nuts, Toasting

Almonds and hazelnuts are often toasted to improve their flavour. Toasting also loosens the dark inner skins of hazelnuts if they are not already peeled.

Heat the oven to gas 4/350°F/180°C. Spread nuts on a baking sheet* or in a roasting tin and bake until lightly browned, stirring occasionally so that they colour evenly. Time varies from 8-15 minutes, depending on whether the nuts are whole or chopped. *Note*: watch carefully as they burn easily.

To remove skins from toasted hazelnuts, rub them while still hot with a rough cloth.

Omelette Pans

Omelette pans can be made of aluminium, cast-iron or stainless steel; the base must be thick to spread heat evenly. Any non-stick surface must resist high heat. To help folding, the sides of the pan should curve at a gentle slope, with handle at an angle.

Pastry Bags and Tubes

Nylon, rather than canvas, is the most practical material for a pastry bag. It should have a waterproof finish. Be sure the slot at the tip of the bag is small enough to hold the tube firmly. Sufficient for most purposes are 2 star tubes for piping* small and medium rosettes, and a selection of plain tubes in sizes from ¼ in/5 mm to ¾ in/2 cm.

Piping

Piping gives a professional touch to many pastries and is almost indispensable for mixtures like Chantilly cream and meringue. The most useful tubes* for pastries are plain and star-shaped (for making rosettes).

Before use, put the required tube in the pastry bag*. Twist the bag just above the tube and push into the tube to block the opening. Hold the bag, tube down, in your left hand and fold about 2 in/5 cm of the bag over your open hand. Gently spoon in the mixture, then unfold the top of the bag and twist it to close, thus pushing the mixture down the tube.

Hold the filled bag in your right hand, keeping the twisted top between thumb and first finger. Use the remaining fingers of your right hand to press the mixture in the bag. With the left hand support the bag without squeezing it. While piping, hold the bag slightly above the surface to be decorated, but do not let them touch.

Poached fruits, see *Fruits*

Praline

For praline made with 3 oz/90 g whole unblanched almonds: oil a baking sheet*. Put almonds in a heavy-bottomed pan with 3 oz/90 g caster sugar. Cook, stirring gently, so that sugar melts and starts to caramelize. Continue cooking until sugar is a deep golden brown and almonds start to pop, showing that they are toasted. Pour mixture on to the baking sheet and leave until cool and crisp. Grind to powder in a food processor or with a rotary cheese grater, or crush as finely as possible with a rolling pin.

Ramekins

The shape of miniature soufflé dishes*, ramekins are used for moulding and for serving a great variety of savoury and sweet dishes. Many are made of plain or decorated porcelain, while unbreakable stainless steel ramekins are the choice for a professional kitchen. For an individual serving, size varies from 4-8 fl oz/125-250 ml, depending on the richness of the mixture.

Ribbon Trail

For preparations such as genoese cake batter and sabayon sauce, whole eggs and sugar are whipped* to a ribbon. When the whisk is lifted, the mixture will form a clear trail which should hold for about 30 seconds. If the trail holds permanently, the mixture is too stiff.

Soft-ball stage, see *Sugar Syrup*

Soufflé Collars

Cold and iced soufflés are moulded with a paper collar so that the mixture extends above the edge of the soufflé dish* and looks as if it has risen in the oven.

Cut a double strip of greaseproof paper or foil (foil is easier to shape) to extend 2-3 in/5-7 cm above the rim of the soufflé dish. Attach it with sticky tape or string.

Soufflé Dishes

The classic soufflé dish is round, with high straight sides so that the mixture rises vertically as it expands. Within this strict definition, there is a wide choice of materials. Traditional is white glazed porcelain fluted on the outside to resemble a pleated paper case. The underside of the dish should be unglazed so that the heat can penetrate quickly. Patterned dishes abound, with animals, birds and vegetable motifs to indicate the contents. Alternatives are glass and earthenware. At a pinch, any straight-sided pan or mould, such as a charlotte mould*, can be used.

Soufflé dishes are always measured by volume as the height of the sides varies. Sizes range from individual ramekins* to 3¼ pt/2 litre dishes serving 8 or more. As a rough guide, 1 egg white occupies 8 fl oz/250 ml of volume in a dish, and serves 1 person.

Spring-form tin, see *Tins*

Sugar Syrup

For 4 fl oz/125 ml caster sugar syrup: put 3 oz/90 g caster sugar in a pan with 4 fl oz/125 ml water and heat until dissolved. Bring to the boil and boil for 3 minutes. This light sugar syrup is useful for moistening cakes. For other recipes a more concentrated syrup, boiled to a specific temperature, is needed.

Soft-ball stage is reached at 239°F/115°C on a sugar thermometer, when syrup forms a soft ball if a little is dropped in cold water.

Hard-ball stage is reached at 248°F/120°C when syrup forms a firm, pliable ball if a little is dropped in cold water.

Hard-crack stage is reached at 294°F/145°C when syrup dropped in cold water hardens at once to a brittle rope which does not stick to the teeth.

Tart tins, see *Tins*

Tartlet tins, see *Tins*

Tins

Tins for cakes and tarts come in a great range of shapes and sizes, but luckily a small number will usually do. Aluminium or stainless steel tins are the most durable as the old-fashioned tinned metal type will start to rust sooner or later. Tins of a blackened steel absorb the heat and therefore brown the contents quickly, while a non-stick finish helps with fruit or nut mixtures which tend to stick.

For cakes, tins should always be lined with a round of greasproof paper. After use, they should not be washed, but wiped out with a damp cloth while still warm. When new, generous buttering helps prevent sticking. In fact a tin sticks less over time as it proves.

Brioche Tins: these are round and deep enough to contain yeast dough as it rises. The sides are sloping and fluted in scallops. Size ranges from about 3 in/7.5 cm for individual brioche tins, to 6-7 in/15-18 cm for large loaves.

Cake Tins: these are generally round, occasionally square or rectangle with straight shallow sides. To make turning out easy, the base should always be lined with greaseproof paper.

Spring-form Tins: these have a loose base and sides attached with a spring-clip. They are used for deep cakes, such as fruit cakes, and for moulding heavy mixtures which are not turned out but slid from the base on to the serving dish.

Tart Tins: these are best with fluted sides and a removable base. Metal flan rings, placed directly on the baking sheet*, can also be used, but be sure that the ring lies flush with the sheet. China tart moulds look attractive but the tart does not brown well and cannot be unmoulded.

Tartlet Tins: these can be large or small, plain or fluted. Deep ones are best for custards and soft fillings, while shallow ones display fruits to advantage.

Tubes, see *Pastry Bags and Tubes*

Water Bath

A water bath or *bain-marie* is used for cooking dishes such as custards, which need a consistently low heat so that they are cooked in the centre without overcooking on the outside. Water baths are also used for melting delicate mixtures and keeping them warm.

Set the cooking dish in a large shallow pan such as a roasting tin and fill with hot water to within 1 in/2.5 cm of the rim of the dish. Bring the water to the boil on top of the stove, then transfer the dish to the water bath to the oven. Start counting the cooking time from the moment the bath is put in the oven.

Whipping Eggs and Sugar

Eggs and sugar, when whipped together, lighten and thicken to form a mousse which is fluffy if made with whole eggs, or close-textured if only egg yolks are used.

Whole eggs (at room temperature) and sugar should be put in a large bowl and whipped with a balloon whisk* or an egg beater to incorporate as much air as possible. If whipping by hand, set the bowl over a pan of hot but not boiling water; if using an electric beater, no heat is necessary. Whip for at least 5 minutes until the mixture is thick and light, forming a ribbon trail*. If whipping by hand, take the bowl from the heat and continue whipping until the mixture is cool.

Egg yolks and sugar should be whipped in a smaller bowl with a sauce whisk, egg beater or electric mixer*, for 3-5 minutes. The mixture will lighten in colour and should be thick enough to hold the mark of the whisk across the bottom of the bowl for a few seconds.

Whipping Egg Whites

Egg whites should be whipped until stiff but not dry. In order for them to whip properly, the whites, bowl and whisk must be completely free from any trace of water, grease or egg yolk. The French prefer to whip egg whites in a copper bowl*, using a balloon whisk* because this achieves greater density and volume than by any other method. The best alternative is to use an electric beater*, preferably with a balloon whisk attachment, and a metal bowl.

Begin by whipping the whites at low speed. When they become foamy and white, increase the speed to maximum, adding a small pinch of salt. The whites are beaten enough when they form a stiff peak when the whisk is lifted, gathering in the whisk and sticking to it without falling. They should be used at once as they quickly separate on standing. If overbeaten, the egg whites become dry and lumpy and cannot be folded together easily with other ingredients.

Whisks and Electric Mixers

Because so many dessert mixtures are whisked, using the right whisk is important. If the aim is a light, fluffy mixture like a mousse, use a balloon-shaped whisk when whisking by hand and lift it half-way out of the mixture as you beat, so that plenty of air is incorporated. On an electric mixer, the whisk attachment is best.

However, if the purpose is to thoroughly combine a mixture, pounding rather than whisking it, a smaller whisk, or sometimes a wooden spatula, is appropriate. The best electric attachment on a mixer is the beater or paddle.

Hand egg-beaters (not used in France) can be used for all purposes, but results with egg whites may be disappointing.

INDEX